WAYS OF THE WOODS:

A Guide to the Skills and Spirit of the Woodland Experience

WAYS OF THE WOODS:

A Guide to the Skills and Spirit of the Woodland Experience

by Moosewood

(Dr. William M. Harlow, Professor of Wood Technology, Emeritus, State University of New York, College of Environmental Science and Forestry)

© Copyright 1979 by The American Forestry Association
1319 Eighteenth Street, N.W.
Washington, D.C. 20036

Library of Congress Catalogue Card No. 79-90432
ISBN-0-935050-00-0

Illustrations by Gordon Mellor
Design by Bob Crozier & Associates

A TRIBUTE
to Dr. William G. Vinal 1881-1976

Before all others, I thank (a feeble word) Dr. William G. "Cap'n Bill" Vinal for directing me into the then-new field of outdoor education, some 50 years ago. He first recommended me to the Society for the Protection of New Hampshire Forests when they were looking for a forester to visit children's summer camps—a kaleidoscope experience if there ever was one! Then followed four summers on the staff of Cap'n Bill's Nature Guide School in Hudson, Ohio. His recommendation took me next to Sargent College of Physical Education's June Camp near Peterborough, NH, where I directed camping and outdoor education for six years. Then to Dr. L.B. Sharp's National Camp for portions of six more summers, where teacher training for school camping was begun—one of the most significant develop-

ments in American education.

This book grew out of those many experiences. Cap'n Bill read and made valuable comments on most of the manuscript. Right up to the end, he still possessed a keen perception and marvelous sense of humor.

So hail and farewell, Old Friend.
With the greatest of affection and admiration,
Moosewood

ACKNOWLEDGEMENTS

Anyone who has ever written a book is well aware that "no man is an island." Literally thousands of people, past and present, have contributed to this book—I am indebted to all of them. Listed below are a few of those who have been especially helpful. During the last four years while I've been writing the book, I'm sure I've failed to record some of those who have made valuable suggestions. To them I apologize, and if I can ever return their help in any way, I hope they'll write me. The names of those credited in the text are not repeated here.

M.M. Alexander, E.A. Anderson, A.H. Bishop, J.A. Barton, D.L. Bennett, Carolyn Corfield, F.E. Carlson, R.A. Cockrell, R.C. Cressey, G.D. Davis, R.C. Deckert, C.H. de Zeeuw, Ralph Drollinger, R.S. Feldman, C.C. Forsaith, George Fuge, L.A. Gorman, Edward Haggerty, D.L. Johnson, Dick Kelty, E.H. Ketchledge, H.F. Lee, Warren Miller, Dorothy O'Brien, Geraldine Owczarzak, J.W. Plant, M.D., V.N. Rockcastle, W.J. Schmidt, J.F. Siau, J.B. Simeone, Christen Skaar, C.F. Smith, G.H. Smith, Kenneth Smith, G.A. Snyder, H.B. Tepper, Fay Welch, K.A. Wherry, H.E. Wilcox.

Over the years, my wife Alma has enthusiastically supported my various projects of books and films. Her skillful, patient hands have appeared in many of the close-up illustrations. I could never find the words that would adequately express what all that has meant to me.

PREFACE

One summer the Society for the Protection of New Hampshire Forests sent me to visit 30 children's camps in 60 days. The purpose was to initiate forestry projects with the children and to advise the director-owners on how to manage their woodlands. I found that many "camps" were surrounded by the forest but were not part of it in any way. At one camp, the counsellors were all college athletes, and their purpose was to coach the boys to excell in high-school sports. A girls camp was devoted to the dance in its various forms and never thought about the forest except as a shady fringe around the campus. As might be expected, each camp was a mirror image of the director and counsellors. I soon learned to size up a camp and its spirit in my preliminary talk with the director. Some of these men and women knew and loved the forest, the adventure contained in woodland trails, the music of crystal-clear brooks, and the amazing impact of the wild environment upon city children, for whom the forest was a new world of mystery and discovery. All summer long these directors kept asking me, "Where will I find counsellors who can interpret nature and who have the skills of the woodsman?" Now that so many teacher colleges have camps that stress the methods of outdoor teaching and knowledge of the woodland environment, one should be able to find people who can serve as counsellors.

This book is for camp directors, counsellors, teachers, and other youth leaders of every kind—but it's also for the millions of people who have been touched by the great environmental movement sweeping the country, and who would like to experience some of the priceless benefits that the forest and other natural areas have to offer.

The repeated claim that the old woodcraft is dead is true only along certain main trails and at campsites where some 10 million backpackers and 50 million day trippers are grinding the wilderness into dust. By contrast, there are millions of acres where you can still explore or camp in the traditional way. These woodlands have been logged at least once, and a luxuriant growth of young trees is springing up. There is plenty of dead firewood and green poles or small logs whose removal only relieves crowding and improves the forest. But know what you are about, and if permission or a fire permit is required, get it.

There are more than 10,000 summer camps run by private owners, "Y", Scouts, school, church, 4-H, and others. Here, camping can still be camping and forest resources can be used properly for building temporary or permanent shelters, for firewood, for craft materials—all on a continuing schedule, year after year. But such conservation is possible only where you have enough land, and, most importantly, where you can control the numbers of campers.

Even though there are a hundred or more new books on camping and outdoor education, I should like to share with you some of the philosophy and techniques I have learned over the last 50 years in association with forestry students, teachers-college people, and many others.

Clearly, this is by no means a "compleat" guide. Many topics are only scanned, mentioned, or omitted entirely. There is appended a list of references ordered alphabetically; notes are listed after each chapter.

A distinguished reviewer read most of my manuscript and penned on the Table of Contents, "It is all camping, woodsmanship, education, and recreation intertwined." Just so. Exploring the outdoors is a way of life, and the topics I've written about and illustrated interconnect to form a web that defies classification.

One of the important principles of the outdoor (environmental) movement is that knowledge and techniques of many confined specialties are fused into vital experiences outside the classroom. I have seen this happen with thousands of students and campers. The Renaissance man who explored everything, and tried to make sense out of life as a whole, has vanished. The explosion of knowledge has rapidly overwhelmed the generalist. To achieve, one has had to specialize, and mathematics, physics, and chemistry have become separate subjects. They now form the "mystic triangle" of the basic sciences upon which everything else is built. As knowledge continues to expand, more and more specialties are spun off until the problems of communication and integration have become tremendous.

Outdoor exploration gives us a chance to "get it all together," though imperfectly, and to view life once again as a whole. The relatively new science of ecology is the key.

CONTENTS

To "L.B."
Woodsman
Pioneer in Outdoor Education
Who Began the School Camping Movement
Colleague and Friend
1895-1963

Dr. L.B. Sharp tending a "buffalo" steak roast.

WHY MOOSEWOOD?

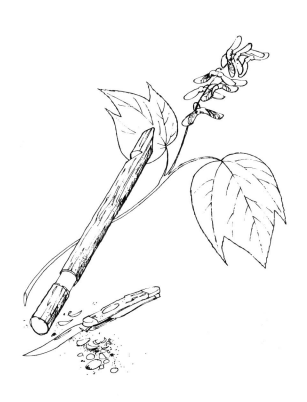

Moosewood Whistles

When John Hollister taught a 12-year-old boy the vanishing art of whistle making in 1913, he could not have foreseen that by this act he was indirectly teaching this thing both pleasing and educational to thousands of people then unborn and now scattered all over the country. One day he came out of his farm woodlot with two of these whistles made of basswood, gave one to me and began playing tunes on the other. Through the years I have met many people who could make a willow whistle, but theirs could play only one note. John Hollister's masterpiece had a sliding plunger so that one could play "Stars and Stripes Forever" and nearly anything else!

Many years later, when I was teaching forestry students tree identification in the Adirondacks,

whistle-making became an informal part of field dendrology. Basswood was very rare, but moosewood (striped maple) was everywhere, and proved to be just as good. At L.B. Sharp's National Camp in New Jersey, during six seasons, nearly 1,000 teachers-college students learned the art with basswood. The faculty dropped formal titles and adopted woodsy ones. At the first campfire, "Cap'n Bill" Vinal introduced me as "Moosewood" and the name has persisted for some 40 years. In fact, some people may think that my middle initial "M" stands for Moosewood.

Whistles can be made only during the growing season when the cambium or growing layer between bark and wood is easily broken by tapping. In the Northeast, this is usually during June and July, although with much trouble I have made whistles in August.

Whenever I felt that camper interest in the outdoors was low in the camps I visited, I strolled into the woods, made a moosewood whistle, came back, sat on a log, and began playing. In less time than it has taken to write this story so far, I always had an audience.

"What's that? Did you make it? Will you make me one?" they'd plead. The answer was always:

"No, I won't make one for you, but I'll show you how to make your own." This was the beginning of a morning's exploration. Those who had pocket knives were taught how to sharpen them (see p. 26). Anything but a keen edge is useless in whistle making.

Then to the woods. I always left a leaf or two on the whistle stick (Fig. 1, No. 1), and the campers searched for leaves that matched on a shrub or small tree with green-and-white striped bark. The name "striped maple" is easy to understand—but why "moosewood"? Here was something for the group to consider. Eventually, someone would say, "Maybe the moose eat it."

"Yes they do," I'd answer, "and so do the deer, who like especially the live twigs in late winter or early spring when other browse is scarce. This often causes several fast-growing sprouts about three-eighths to one-half inch in diameter to shoot up—just what we want for whistles. Before you cut all the sprouts, look around. Are there any other moosewoods nearby? If not, leave a couple of the shoots with their leaves to make food for the plant."

All this should suggest some stimulating

questions to ask, including: "Why shouldn't we cut down the whole thing?" A single shoot may make two or three whistles. What you need is a smooth, nearly cylindrical section free of side branches for about three inches. Hold the shoot with its top away from you, and make a clean 30-to-40-degree cut severing the shoot below a pair of side branches, where the diameter is no greater than that down along the stem to the next pair of leaves, which can be cut off. About four inches below this point, cut the shoot in two. You now have your whistle "blank." (No. 2.) (If you don't have much whittling experience and wish to try this yourself, you should first read how to whittle in the chapter on "A Camper's Tools," starting page 25.)

Hold your thumb safely below the end of the stick top with the slanted surface toward you, and make a paring cross-cut about a quarter-inch from the end. This makes a typical whistle mouthpiece. About a half-inch from the new end, on top, make a cross-wise cut about one-third through, followed by a very clean diagonal cut slanting down to the bottom of the first cut. This frees a wedge of bark and wood. Now go down the whistle blank about three inches, and very carefully ring the bark with a cut that frees it but does not go into the wood.

If your knife has a smooth handle, hold the blade carefully with the edge away from you, place the whistle on something smooth and solid, and gently tap the entire outer surface, starting at the top and working around and around until you come to the cut ring at the bottom. This has to be done firmly but carefully, especially at the mouthpiece top where the bark is most easily broken. After some five minutes, grasp the whistle halfway down and with the other hand carefully twist just a little at the top end. If you feel the bark slip you are in luck. Perhaps you can work this twist down to the bottom and the whole hollow cylinder of bark will turn freely on the wood. If not, keep tapping and twisting until it does. Now pull this sleeve off (No. 3). Very carefully flatten the wood end on top to provide an air channel. Too little flattening will make the volume of sound very small, but too much will make a harsh sound or even none at all. Carefully cut the wood around and around where the first notching cut was made. All of a sudden the little end plug may fly off and get lost in the leaves. Keep a sharp eye so this doesn't happen. Pick it up, and slip it back into the bark sleeve. (Incidentally, I discovered while thumbing through the dictionary recently that the little end plug has a name: "fipple"!) Start slipping the plunger back and forth as you blow gently on the mouthpiece. Keep the plunger lubricated with saliva.

With this woodsy slide-whistle you can do lots of things—including bird calls, especially that of the white-throated sparrow. In the United States he says, "Oh Sam Peabody, Peabody, Peabody" but as soon as he crosses the Canadian border it's, "Oh sweet Canada, Canada, Canada!" How many other species besides basswood and moosewood can you use? I do not know, but I have used fast-growing shoots of red maple. What you need is a shrub or tree that has a tough bark and long, cylindrical sprouts. After the first enthusiasm has abated, try asking your group to experiment and see how the length of the air column determines the pitch. These whistles are miniature organ pipes and work on the same principle.

Fig. 1: The Moosewood Whistle. 1) Leaves on cylindrical sprout. 2) First stage. 3) Bark sleeve slipped off after tapping and twisting. 4) Flattened and separated end. 5) Assembled whistle. 6) "Moosewood."

INTRODUCTION TO ORGANIZED CAMPING

Unless you have lived in our country from 1900 to the present, you can hardly sense the enormous changes that have taken place in the way we live. Prior to this century, the world was very different. Most Americans lived on farms or in small villages. There was no radio or television, only a few primitive automobiles, no air transport, no ICBM's: in fact almost nothing that shapes our lives today. Many years ago, my old aunt born in the 1860s said to me, "Sometimes when I look around and see all the things that have happened during my lifetime, I feel as if I've lived a thousand years!" And so she had, in terms of previous human technology.

Country children were needed to help with farm work during the long summer vacation from school. Actually, this work was an important part of

their education, whether or not they suspected it. City children played in the streets. The few who had affluent parents might go with them to "primitive" woodland hotels or to the seashore.

The population pattern of our country over the past century has changed radically. Most children are now brought up in big cities—only relatively few grow up on farms. The changes in lifestyle of city children housed in highrise apartments have made a good camping experience much more important than it might have been many years ago. This was a concern even in the 1880s, when "Nessmuk," or George Washington Sears, wrote perhaps the first book on camping. His *Woodcraft* is a fascinating story of travel by foot and canoe through the wilderness of a century ago. I quote a verse from that book:

> For brick and mortar breed filth and crime,
> With a pulse of evil that throbs and beats;
> And men are withered before their prime
> By the curse paved in with the lanes and streets.
>
> And lungs are poisoned and shoulders bowed,
> In the smothering reek of mill and mine;
> And death stalks in on the struggling crowd—
> But he shuns the shadow of oak and pine.[1]

This may shock some of you—and admittedly, progress is being made to improve city environments—but unfortunately for millions of our people, these verses still ring true.

Organized camping seems to have been an American creation. Between 1880 and 1900, a score of boys camps were started, but only one—famous YMCA Camp Dudley on Lake Champlain—is still fulfilling its original purpose of character-building in the out-of-doors. Like many other camps, Dudley started small. During the summer of 1885, Sumner F. Dudley, a dedicated leader who loved the woods, took six Newburgh, New York boys camping. The number increased, and by 1891 there were 83 campers. After the untimely death of Mr. Dudley, the camp was named for him, and the "Dudley spirit" became a tradition. By 1902, the enrollment was 226, and the camp had evolved to the typical centralized or campus arrangement. As the camping movement gathered momentum, "graduates" from Dudley were in demand as directors and counsellors, and they helped to shape the philosophy, organization, and programs of these new camps.[2]

I'm familiar with the centralized camp—I was a camper in one, have directed a couple of them, and I've visited some 50 others. Although there are many variations, in each camp you will probably find a grassy opening with a flagpole in the center, and tents grouped around the outside of the opening. Did I say *tents*? At some point in the evolution of many camps, these have been replaced with electrically lighted cabins for the "comfort and welfare" of the campers! May I say that you no longer have a camp, but rather a rural hamlet? The valuable experience of living under canvas is lost if you live in a house, even though it's out in the woods.

The centralized camp has a large professionally run kitchen and dining hall where perhaps 100 or more children eat their meals. Outdoor small-group cooking may be unheard of. This kind of camp is departmentalized, with specialists in charge of each activity—waterfront, several kinds of field sports, dramatics, trips away from camp, crafts (mostly with kits of "artificial" stuff ordered from a catalog), nature and woodcraft (maybe), and others.

To operate a large organization like this, there must be a regular schedule, with some activity planned for almost every waking moment of a camper's day. The beginning of each "class" or "period" is signalled by a bell or bugle.

Through the years, more and more "camps" have been formed with the purpose of teaching a single specialty. This trend was well under way even in the late 1920s, when I visited 30 of the New Hampshire camps that existed then. One of them purposed only to teach its girls various forms of the dance. At a boys camp, each counsellor was a college athlete, an expert in one particular sport. Every boy was there to be coached so that he could make the school team back home. The atmosphere was highly competitive—it was all a very serious business.

These examples should show how far the camping movement has departed from its simple beginnings. Remember that Mr. Dudley and his six boys went camping together in the woods. It was an *environmental experience.*

The original Life Magazine in 1887 began raising funds to send selected New York City slum children out to the farm for a few weeks each summer. The several farms evolved into camps, and these followed the usual pattern. They were centralized, regimented, had "classes" in various "subjects," played competitive sports, and offered awards to the winners.

In 1926, Dr. L.B. Sharp, the Life Camps'

Executive Director—a keen observer of human growth and values—came to a decision. The camps were simply not fulfilling the needs of these city children. He decided to throw the whole kit and kaboodle overboard and to go back to beginnings. He believed that each child, as part of a small group, should have the chance to live in and explore the forest instead of just repeating the forms of recreation already to be found in city playgrounds.

L.B. later told me how he began in his older-boys camp. One day after lunch he drifted over to one of the tents and said, "How would you guys like to go pioneering out there in the woods? We could let you have a couple of tarps for shelter, an axe and saw, and some other things. You could plan your own menus, and get your supplies at the wannigan [kitchen]. Later in the afternoon, you could come down for a swim, and then eat supper with the others. Afterward, you could go back to your forest camp, and sit around your own campfire before turning in."

It didn't take the boys long to fall for the idea. One said, "Sure, let's try it, it might be fun!" So, with their counsellor—a man of experience who'd been enthused by L.B.—they spent a couple of days exploring to find a good campsite. Then they moved out and began a totally new experience, living in the woods. Naturally, the other boys were curious about what was going on. When they saw the pioneers bubbling over with delight, they all said, "Hey, why not us too?" And so, eventually, the whole camp program changed.

When I visited the camp in the early '40s, the old tent platforms and frames arranged in military company street formation were still there, some canvas-covered for visitors, storage, etc. Otherwise, all was quiet. Where were the boys? L.B. took me on a tour along narrow, winding woodland trails to about six little camps scattered throughout the forest. Each one showed the creativity of its builders, and no two were alike. Through the years, several types of unique shelters were invented.

Dr. Sharp was to write later: "Decentralized camping involves the organization of campers into small family groups of eight or nine including two co-leaders. Each unit is responsible, as far as possible, for its own program, welfare, and way of camping. Each unit becomes a small camp that has a life, a unity, and a character of its own, but receives guidance and leadership from the directorship of the whole camp."

At the same time that Life's Camp for Boys was evolving into the small groups, the Life Girls Camp was going through almost exactly the same creative process. Groups were soon filing "land claims" for new campsites as excitedly as pioneers in the Oklahoma land rush. The groups burst out of the small acreage of their first camp, and the entire camp was forced to find a new location on a thousand-acre tract in northwestern New Jersey. Lois Goodrich, working with L.B. Sharp from those early beginnings of decentralization, has successfully directed the Girls Camp and later both Boys and Girls Camps—now called Trail Blazer Camps—at the same site for nearly half a century.[3]

I recently read an article in Camping magazine suggesting that in this environmental era, we should have more "land and forest-centered programs." It's not a new idea!

The biggest problem is to find and train counsellors who know the outdoors and the skills needed. Lois devotes two weeks each June to a thorough staff-training program. She uses her experienced staff as key people during the training in outdoor living and group problem solving. It's an enormous challenge for the counsellors to sit down with their eight city children that first evening around the campfire, in the silent darkening forest. Half of them the first night, and half the second, are encouraged to tell their personal stories—family, background, interests, etc. This is not only a cure for homesickness, but of great value to the other campers. Each one has his own unique contribution to make, and each is important to the group. The sociological implications of this kind of small-group living are tremendous.

The small-group camp has none of the noise, uproar, high competition, and tensions found in the "traditional" large, centralized camp. From day to day, each group's two counsellors (one experienced, the other less so) help the children plan their own program. They may elect to cook and eat one or two meals at their small camp and have the third meal at the main dining hall, which is rarely filled. They can plan all kinds of explorations, perhaps to a nearby quaking peat bog, or (using a camp vehicle) to a day's mountain-climbing adventure. The waterfront—with its activities of swimming, boating, and canoeing—functions as usual, except that congestion is avoided by serving just several of the small group camps at a time instead of the whole camp population. Staff counsellors with their specialties visit the small camps and find great satisfaction in working with small groups.

Periodic evening campfires in the Council Ring bring the entire camp together for songs, Amer-Indian dancing and games, nature reports or questions by the campers on what they've seen, and storytelling. Of course, the success of these gatherings depends upon the skill of the "Chief" or camp director who can transform the occasion into a magical experience.

There are, of course, other kinds of camping and woodland experiences. Hundreds of camps build their programs around canoe trips through the magnificent northern wilderness, where glaciers have left uncounted thousands of ponds and lakes interconnected by unpolluted silver streams. The horse often replaces the canoe, especially in the West.

The tremendous development of school camping begun by L. B. Sharp in the '40s has opened the eyes of millions of youngsters to the ultimate adventure of "going home"—back to the primitive environment from which we all came. Apart from camping opportunities, thousands of "nature centers" are springing up not only to serve schools but to aid the whole environmental movement.

People who go to the greenwood should have a basic understanding of it, and should know how to behave themselves there for their own enjoyment and safety and those of others. Some of these basics are contained in the following chapters. They're important, whether you spend a few hours along a woodland trail or head out on a several-day backpacking expedition.

INTRODUCTION TO ORGANIZED CAMPING
1. Page 4—Nessmuk (G.W. Sears), *Woodcraft*. New York: Dover, 1963.
2. Page 4—For a more complete description of the founding of Camp Dudley, see Minott A. Osborn's book *Camp Dudley—The First Fifty Years* (New York: Huntington Press, 1934). It tells a fascinating story of growth and development.
3. Page 6—I'm quite aware that over the years decentralized camping has been developed by organizations other than Life Camps. I used the Life Camps (now independent) only as the example I know best. For a discussion of this subject, get Lois Goodrich's *Decentralized Camping* (New York: Association Press, 1959) from the library—unfortunately, it's out of print at this time.

NATIONAL CAMP TARP SHELTERS

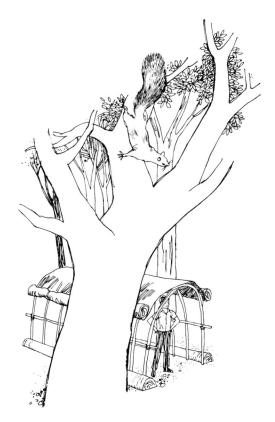

The common kinds of tents (A-tent, army pyramidal tent, and others) used for many years in semi-permanent camps are too well-known to be discussed.[1]

Dr. Sharp's several camps developed some unique shelters using standard-size, brown, waterproof canvas tarps. Fig. 2, No. 1 shows the primitive construction of a hogan. A ship's auger was used to bore a row of large holes spaced along the base logs. Into these holes were fitted long limber hardwood saplings, which were then bent, overlapped, and tied. A ridgepole, horizontal rail, and diagonal braces completed the structure, Along each edge of the rolled-down cover, a long pole was tied. Thus the cover could be propped outward with forked sticks to give more light and air, or on sunny days rolled partway up and tied to the frame. The canvas

extended about six inches beyond each end hoop, and a pair of vertical end-curtains were tied at the top and along the sides. The whole thing was built to shelter four camp beds, with additional storage space at each end.

At National Camp, which had a sawmill and plenty of oak timbers, a more permanent variation on this shelter was used. Heavy 8 x 8 timbers supported an oaken floor, and along the edges, spiked 4 x 4's were drilled to take the ends of the bent saplings. (It's a good idea to pour creosote or other wood preservative into the holes.) The 8 x 8's had sloping ends so that a tractor could skid the platform from one place to another. It was an oversize "stone boat" like that used with teams of oxen by the early settlers to rid the fields of boulders and smaller stones. At National these shelters were called "sleds"; you'd sometimes hear someone say, "I'll meet you up at my sled right after lunch."

Fig. 2, No. 2 shows a group of inner-city youngsters—out in the woods for the first time—building another kind of tarp-covered shelter, the "round-to." Note the heavy back-log, in front of which the ends of the saplings are firmly bedded into the ground. Above this, another, smaller "log" is firmly lashed at the ends. The vertical saplings are *behind* this second log. When the framework is completed, the upper ends are trimmed even with the top crosspiece, and then strong ropes are used to slowly pull the structure into a curve with the forward edge, perhaps five feet from the ground. The rope ends are tied to deeply driven stakes. There's considerable tension in this structure until it gets set. Canvas-covered, with end curtains, and with a bright little fire in front, it makes a snug forest home indeed.

With these two shelters, and with others that you and your campers may invent, what will you use for lashings? There's nothing as good or as cheap as binder twine purchased from farm-supply distributors. The breaking strength is about 100 pounds—a safe working load is 30 pounds. The color blends with the environment, and it's bio-degradable. After two years it probably should be replaced—a distinct advantage. It's more fun and better education to build something yourself than simply to use a shelter made by someone else. You may want to change the design or replace some of the poles. At the beginning of the third summer, the dry hardwood poles make excellent firewood, but if left too long, they'll begin to decay, especially at the butt ends. You may be

7

tempted to buy the more expensive and much stronger nylon cord for lashings. Don't do it. Besides the fact that it virtually lasts forever, its various bright colors pollute the greenwood.

NATIONAL CAMP TARP SHELTERS

1. Page 7—Trail tents are discussed by William Kemsley Jr. and the editors of Backpacker Magazine in *Backpacking Equipment Buyer's Guide*, New York: Collier Macmillan, 1977.

Fig. 2: Tarp Shelters. 1) Hogan with canvas rolled back, showing construction. 2) "Round-to" building. The forked stick at right and other vertical supports are temporary until horizontal poles are lashed. (Photo by Trail Blazers Camps)

THE AMERINDIAN TIPI AND WILLOW BED

The Tipi

The tipi of the Plains Indians is the most beautiful and functional portable home ever invented by primitive man. No modern-day permanent camp is complete without at least one of these lodges. When the tipi is erected in the woods, one can become spellbound watching the moving patterns of light and shadow cast upon the white canvas by the leaves and branches high overhead. With the slightest breeze, the patterns are put in constant motion. As the sun moves across the sky, its angle keeps changing daily, so that the patterns are never quite the same from one day to the next. (Those who know *tipi* as *tepee* might consider that in the Sioux tongue "ti" means "dwelling" and "pi" signifies "used for." Since "i" is pronounced "ee" we have tepee in English.)

Many kinds of primitive dwellings have a simple smoke hole at the top. This is never very efficient. The genius of the tipi's inventor is shown by the extension of the cover on both sides at the top to form movable flaps, each held aloft by its pole. On the plains, the tipi was faced to the east. When the flaps were placed almost parallel, they acted as a chimney and provided a draft so that smoke from the fire below did not collect in the lodge but was carried out through the smoke hole by the prevailing westerly winds. When the wind shifted, the flaps were moved to one side or the other, so that the opening between them continued to face away from the wind. In many modern-day camps that have tipis, few counsellors have any idea what these smoke flaps are for. Usually one finds them spread out on the sides like sails, in which position they are all but useless.

Inside the tipi, a little back of the center, the fire pit has been dug about six inches deep, and is surrounded at ground level by stones. The tipi fire is always small, both because of safety, and because a larger one would soon roast the dwellers out, so efficient are the tipi walls in reflecting the heat. Although coniferous woods can be burned, most of them, especially hemlock, often throw out hot embers. Woods of the broadleaf trees, with few exceptions, are preferred. Any wood burned in a tipi fire should be as dry as possible. It is asking too much of the ventilators to take out the heavy smoke from a fire built partly with wet wood.

How the tipi happened to be invented is lost in the mists of time. Perhaps someone twisted a cottonwood leaf into a cone and saw it as a miniature lodge. Indian children did in fact make such play tipis from cottonwood leaves. Originally, the tipi was a shelter for spring, summer, and early autumn, when the tribes were roaming on foot in search of buffalo. It was a hunting lodge, only about 10 feet high with slender, lightweight poles. For travel, the poles were bunched together and harnessed to the only beast of burden the Indians had at first—the dog. In this way the poles were dragged along, the butt ends on the ground, from one campsite to the next. During the colder months, the tribes lived in octagonal dugouts some 20 feet across, roofed with poles covered by sod and packed earth. There was a slanting downhill entrance, and a central smoke hole.

But all this was to change with the introduction of the horse. The Sioux, Crow, Dakota, Omaha,

Blackfoot, and others would become the lords of the Great Plains. Imagine the astonishment of the first Indian who saw the first horse, and how he must have schemed to be its master. Coronado came north through present-day New Mexico in 1541 in search of the fabled cities of gold. With a band of 30 horsemen, he crossed the Texas panhandle and rode to the great bend of the Arkansas River in central Kansas. Finding nothing of value, he turned back. Were they observed by the Indians? Did the news spread like wildfire of gods riding great beasts that ran like the wind? During the next century, wild bands of horses were roaming the plains, and the Indians began their great adventure with them.

Besides having a new means with which to hunt bison, the Indians now had a way of dragging tipi poles 25 to 40 feet long if necessary. Virtually overnight, the small hunting tipi became a magnificent lodge, usually about 18 feet in height and diameter, but sometimes reaching 25 feet or more.

Nature cooperated with an unlimited supply of long, slender poles from the lodgepole pine of the Rocky Mountains. Unlike most pines, this one produces many cones that do not open when ripe. As the years pass, thousands of cones containing millions of viable seeds accumulate. When a fire races through a lodgepole forest, the layer of old needles on the ground is burned along with the smaller branches and live needles on the trees. Resins that have held the cone scales together sputter and burn in the intense heat, but the cones open only a little. Very soon, the fire moves on, and as the cones cool, the scales open and out slip the winged seeds—millions and millions of them. The cooling, bare earth is just what they need for germination. In a few years there is a dense stand of young slender pole-size trunks ready for the taking.

The poles were always cut three to six feet longer than needed, both for looks, and because the butt ends dragging on the ground from camp to

Fig. 3: Tipi of the Plains Indians in a woodland setting.

camp continually shortened the poles until they were useless. Each spring, when the bark peeled easily, the tribes made the long trek up into the mountains to get a new set of poles. The old ones might still do, but it was risky to use them for another year.

The early writers soon found that the Indian man knew nothing about cutting the poles, preparing and sewing together the buffalo hides, and erecting the tipi. This was all squaws' work, and the women took great pride in it. The peeled poles were scraped until glass smooth. Not a single protruding branch end, not a single shaving or whisker was tolerated. Protruding branch ends would wear a hole in the cover, and when it rained something else might happen. Rain runs down the poles along their undersides to the ground. But if there are projections, then at each one there is a steady drip—perhaps on you or your bed!

And what can we moderns use for poles? There are now vast plantations of young pines scattered throughout the land, many of them of pole size and in need of thinning to prevent stagnation of growth. As soon as the bark will peel in the spring, go to it. If some of the poles are not quite straight, they can be tightly bundled and left to dry. All poles must be air dried, preferably in the sun, before use. For a 16-foot tipi, you will need 18 to 20 poles of random length (18-20 feet) about 2½ to 3½ inches in diameter at the butt, and one inch at the top. The butts are pointed so they can be pushed into the ground for greater stability. If you are in a young forest of broadleaf trees, pole hunting will take more time, and the poles, although usable, may not be as straight as those of the conifers. Another possibility, although not "woodsy," is to use bamboo poles. I have used them, but they are so light in weight that the pole structure is not too stable, and the end of a long rope from the tripod tie must always be fastened to a ground stake inside the tipi.

Only the aristocracy—that is, the chiefs and medicine men—had painted tipis which represented the religious art of the Plains Indians. The top of the Blackfoot tipi was painted black to represent the night sky. Arrangements of white circles, especially on the smoke flaps, represented constellations. Two favorites were the Great Bear (Big Dipper), and the Pleiades (Seven Little Sisters). Circling the tipi just below the black top were concentric yellow or orange bands signifying the sunrise. Along the painted band at the bottom were one or two rows of white circles that represented the giant white puffballs of edible fungi, some as big as one's head, often found on the plains. The Indians called them "fallen stars." Above them was a row of pointed teeth—hills or mountains. Behind, opposite the door and below the yellow sunrise bands, was a green or blue maltese cross, interpreted either as the moth or sleep bringer, or as the morning star.

Most painted tipis showed this general design, but this was just the beginning. To the Indian family, especially the Blackfoot, pictographs of animals and hunting exploits—shown around the tipi below the sunrise bands and above the mountains—were most important. They signified that supernatural powers protected a tipi and its family. The buffalo had the most power, but the deer and elk were also great; so were the eagle and raven. Among the "underwater people," the beaver was chief, but the otter was also very strong. Each tipi had an exclusive design given in a dream to the owner. Not only could it not be copied by anyone else, but there could be only one tipi at a time bearing this pattern. When the tipi cover got too worn, it was sacrificed to the sun by weighting it with rocks and sinking it in a pond or lake. Then a new cover was painted with the sacred design.

Every summer there were great-circle encampments to celebrate the sun dance. The ordinary tipis, perhaps some 350 of them, formed an outer circle nearly a mile in circumference. Inside was another, much smaller circle of painted tipis. The few white men privileged to visit one of these great encampments never forgot the experience. At night an outside observer beneath a star-studded sky would see the fire-lighted designs from within the great lodges as things of beauty circling the dark prairie. Perhaps on a calm cloudless night, a sleeping paleface visitor might be wakened by the sound of tapping as the squaws drove deeper the circles of stakes that held down the tipi covers. Two or three hours later a fierce wind would sweep across the camp. When asked how she knew the wind was coming, a squaw might shrug, or say, "Ky-o-te tell me."

The Indians were dependent upon game, especially the buffalo, and when the animals moved on, so did the tribe. The night before moving, a herald rode around the tipi circle, calling out, "The grass is short, wood is scarce, the water is stale, and the game has gone. We move tomorrow." In the morning, at a signal from the chief's tipi, all the other tipis came down within a few minutes, and in no time at all, the whole village was moving away across the prairie.

All this is gone forever, but you can sample what it must have been like by painting and erecting your own tipi and then living in it. During a sunny day in the woods, you can lie on your bed and watch the dancing shadows of leaves and branches against the white tipi cover. At night you can marvel at the flickering shadows cast by the small fire in the center, and share with primitive man an experience that may go back several hundred years.

For cold-weather use especially, you need an inner lining attached to the poles inside the tipi. As Reginald and Gladys Laubin say in their book *The Indian Tipi,* without this lining, the tipi is often a drafty affair. They have made and spent much time in tipis, including winters with temperatures of 20° below zero. I leave it to them to tell you about the inner lining or "dewcloth," as well as many other things about the tipi, and of the lives of the oldtime Plains Indians.[1]

To Set Up a Tipi

"Ingredients":
11 sharpened pegs, of equal length (1-2 feet)
1 eight-foot cord
1 tipi cover (Order one from Select Service Supply Company, 2905 E. Amwiler Rd., Atlanta, GA 30360. Send for a catalog.)
18-20 pine poles, 18-20 feet long, 2½-3½ inches diameter at butt, one inch at top, peeled and scraped
quarter-inch manila rope
half-inch manila rope
1 crayon
Lacing pins, one for each set of grommet holes
Inside lining (optional)

1. At the slightly raised, levelled, smoothed, packed-down tipi site, mark a circle in the ground. If using the standard 16-foot size (diameter along straight edge), drive a peg into the ground about where you want the center of the tipi to be. With another sharpened peg, and an eight-foot cord, mark out a 16-foot-diameter circle for an approximate guide in placing the butts of the tripod poles. Distance from the center to the door pole will be a little more than that to the other two poles. This puts the door pole perhaps a foot or so outside your circle. Only practice gets it just right.

2. Lay the cover out smoothly on adjacent level ground, with the outside up. If decorated, you can tell easily—if not, look for the seams, which should be turned under.

3. Put aside temporarily two of the longest poles for raising the smoke flaps. Then choose three of the strongest, largest poles for the tripod.

4. Lay two of them side by side, on top of the cover, dividing it into halves, with the large ends of the poles about two inches beyond the curve of the canvas, and the small (top) ends extending on top of and past the tie flap in the center of the cover's straight edge.

5. Pick up the third pole and lay it to the right with the small end crossing the other two and the butt end about one-third of the way down from the straight edge (Fig. 4, No. 1). The butt end should extend about two inches beyond the edge of the cover, as do the other two poles. This third pole is the door pole, which will face east.

6. Now take about five feet of ¼-inch Manila rope and make a clove hitch around the poles as shown (No. 2 and No. 3). Follow this with several snug turns and finish with a square knot. Be sure the tie goes from lower left to upper right, or the poles won't lock properly when spread to form the tripod. If the tipi is used in the open, a second tie rope of ½-inch manila is fastened over the first tie. This line is long enough so that the lower end can be fastened to a stout stake driven into the ground about one-third of the way from the fireplace to the back of the tipi. In the woods, this defense against the wind is usually not necessary.

7. Assuming that you have spread out the cover on flat open ground nearby, you may have to carry the tripod poles along a narrow woodland trail to the tipi circle. If so, the single door pole must be swung to lie parallel along the other two poles. This may loosen the tie rope, so mark each pole with a crayon so you can slip the tie back to position if it slides up or down on the poles. Better yet, also use a temporary tie to keep the poles in carrying position. Two or three people should hold the poles together and carry them to the tipi circle. Remove the "carrying tie." Now the door pole is swung to its original position on top of the other two, and facing east. The poles are then raised, with one person anchoring the end of the door pole with his foot, while one or two others lift and spread the two remaining poles to form the tripod. If, at the tie, you lift the three poles so that you look toward their bases, then the *righthand*

pole of the *two parallel* poles must be pulled toward you to "lock" the binding at the top. These two poles have their base ends approximately in the tipi circle. The base of the door pole is a little outside of it.

8. Now, starting at the door pole, slide the other spaced poles up into the tripod, keeping their bases about two feet inside the tipi circle. Try to place four poles to the right, and then another four poles to the left of the door pole; at least two or three of the poles on each side should rest in the front fork. This makes the least possible number under the top of the cover, for best fit. Finally, the rear poles are fitted in, with a space left for the lifting pole. If this space is planned just right, then when the cover is unrolled, the door will be *between* the door pole and the one next to it.

9. Now go back to the tipi cover lying on the ground. Take a large, strong pole and slide its top *under* the curved edge at the center, and up so that the top lies under the tie flap, and the base of the pole extends about four inches beyond the cover's curved edge.

10. Tie the small flap securely to this "lifting pole."

11. A group of four to six people spaced evenly (two or three on each side of center) along the straight edge now begins to roll the cover inward (one or two can do it, but it takes longer). The two on each side of the center must roll very slowly to allow those below to keep the cover rolling in a straight line. Each side rolls until both meet evenly at the lifting pole. Pass a short line around the base of the rolled canvas and pole, and tie it snugly. Do the same thing half-way up. Several people now shoulder canvas and pole, and proceed to the tipi circle. The Indians made radial folds in the cover instead of rolling, but control of the bulky canvas seems easier with the method described.

12. Two or three people now carry the lifting pole with its rolled canvas around to the rear space left for it, and slide its top up into the cluster of other poles, fitting it in snugly. The pole's base is in the marked tipi circle.

13. Untie the two lines holding canvas to pole, and carefully unroll the cover around the poles until the two edges meet and overlap in front.

14. Line up the grommet holes, and starting at the top, slide in the lacing pins. These are slender peeled wands, or dowels about 16 inches long, pointed on the ends. Each pin goes straight through two grommets on one side, then across inside, and out through the other two. The pointed ends of the pins now show in a double row up and down the front of the tipi. Doing this for the top pins requires a "little Indian" standing on the shoulders of a "big Indian," or you may make a two-step ladder by lashing short poles horizontally between the door pole and one next to it.

15. Now go all the way around inside the tipi and carefully push each pole outward until the cover is smooth and tight, without a wrinkle anywhere. This will take some practice. The door pole is sometimes found to be too long for a good cover fit. Even the Indians have been seen either to chop off the base end or bury it deeper in the ground, whichever is easier.

16. Around the bottom of the tipi are grommets with rope ties. When the tipi is erected in the open, strong stakes are driven into the ground at these points and the ropes are tied to them. On a hot day with little wind, the tipi cover should be rolled *inward* and upward all around, leaving an air space for ventilation. In the woods, staking may not even be needed—but better do it anyway. The cover should not touch the ground at any point around the circle.

17. Now for the two extra-long smoke-flap poles. A pole slipped into the pocket of each flap raises it. By moving the poles, you can change the position of your chimney. The flaps should be parallel or slightly spread. When the opening faces away from the wind, the smoke from the small fire in the center is drawn out of the tipi. A drainage trench should go around the outside edge of the cover. If the two poles are found to be too long for convenience, they may be shortened a little.

These directions may sound complicated, but really they are not. It was said that a squaw could put up a tipi in two or three minutes, a seemingly impossible feat!

The Willow Bed

Not only did the Plains Indian have the most beautiful and practical lodge—he also slept on a healthful and comfortable bed made of some 150 willow rods cleverly strung together (Fig. 5, No. 1). When not in use, the bed was rolled up for carrying. Without the head and foot pieces, it weighs about seven pounds. Considering the fragile appearance of the willow bed, it may seem remarkable that it comfortably supports a 175-pound man; but this it does, the rods bending just the right amount so that the entire body is comfortably supported from head to foot.

Do not sit near the center, between the poles; the willows are not strong enough. Rather, sit carefully over one of the poles, and then quickly roll onto the bed with your body fully extended. Ah! A new sensation of comfortable support unlike any you've ever had before. When I introduce the willow bed—as I've done to hundreds of campers through the years —the first one to try it sighs delightedly and with a pleased smile looks up to the arching trees overhead and says, "I guess I'll just stay here all day!"

Making a willow bed is a good group project. It requires about 150 rods for a six-foot bed, not counting the head or foot pieces, which are optional. If not enough willows can be found, other common straight-growing native shrubs such as arrowwood (viburnum) and red-stemmed dogwood can be used. If you want, you can easily make a willow plantation (basket willow works best) by cutting two-foot willow lengths and planting the base ends in moist soil where there is little or no shade. One hundred or more pieces, planted 1½ feet apart and about eight inches deep, will give you a thicket useful not only for willow beds but for basket weaving and other nature crafts as well.

Fig. 4: Erecting a model four-foot tipi. 1) Door pole, about one-third of the way from straight-edge to center of curved cover. 2) Clove hitch around pole crossing. 3) Finished binding. 4) Rolled cover and lifting pole. 5) Partly unrolled cover. 6) Cover pinned and poles spread.

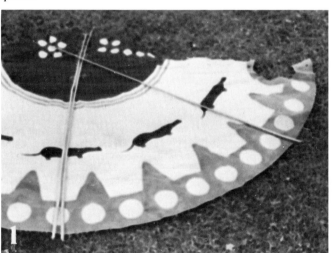
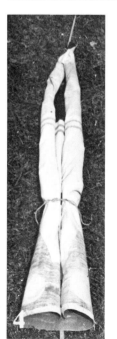

Whatever rods you use for your willow bed should have few if any side branches, and they should be cut early in the season when they can be peeled easily. Choose rods at least 5/16-inch in diameter at the top and half an inch or less at the bottom; they should be cut about 34 inches in length. Peeled rods are rarely straight—make them so by bending them. Then take a dozen or so at a time and bundle and tie them tightly at several places to make them dry straight.

When you have enough dry rods, they should be trimmed at both ends with a fine saw to an exact length of 33 inches. Now the rods are drilled with 1/16-inch holes, three eighths of an inch from each rod end; or you may burn the holes with a red-hot nail. Two three-foot cross logs are staked about six feet two inches apart. On top of each log, drive four nails partly in. The nails at each end should be 32¼ inches apart. The other two are equally spaced between the end pair. Leaving about a foot of extra line at each tie, connect each pair of end nails to their partners on the other log, using lengths of heavy fishline or other cord. The center two nails are likewise connected with lengthwise cords, only these are *double,* and are about 13 feet long. All these lengthwise cords should be of about the same tautness.

To weave the bed start at the head. Select one of your largest, strongest rods. Pass it crosswise *under* the single cord on one side, and between each pair of double cords as you go along until the rod ends lies *under* the lengthwise cord on the other side (No. 2 and No. 3). Push the rod against the nails. Take two three-foot pieces of strong fishline thin enough to pass easily through the holes in the rod ends. Between the nails and the rod at each end, tie one end of each of the two pieces of fishline very securely to the lengthwise cords. At each end of the rod, pass the free end of fishline through the hole in the rod and *around* the lengthwise cord (No. 2). Now slide the second rod alongside the first, and *cross* the double cords as you go (No. 3). At each end of the rod, pass the fishline through the hole as before and around the lengthwise cords on each side of the bed. Alternate the large butt ends with the smaller top ends as you proceed, so as to keep the length of the bed uniform. After you have a few rods strung in place, you will need to take up the slack on each side, so that everything is snug. You will now see that the fishline spirals around the outside cords, passing through and binding a rod end at each turn.

Presently, you will use up the spiralling fishline—so just tie on another piece of convenient length, and keep going. If some of your rods seem a trifle small, save them for the lower two feet of the bed. Also save one stout rod to finish off the foot. As you cross the double strands each time a new rod is added, they get tighter as they shorten. When the tension gets greater than that of the side cords, loosen the double cords a little at the foot. This slowly uses up the extra footage. When you finally bind on the last rod, tie the double cords around it and cut them off.

The two supporting side poles, resting in forked stakes at each end, should be large and stiff enough so that they bend very little under the weight of the sleeper. How much closer together should the poles be than the width of the bed? Try five inches, giving the bed an overlap of 2½ inches on each side. The wider the poles, the more comfortable the bed —but so is there also more danger of the bed slipping off inside the poles. This may be disastrous to the bed, and not comforting to you! Place the rolled-up bed across the poles at one end, and tie the ends of the two lengthwise cords to the forked stakes. Then unroll the bed and stretch it tight, tying the cord ends as before. At two points one-third the distance from each end, there should be a tie on each side of the bed to fasten it to the poles. This is further insurance that one edge of the bed will not slide too far to one side or the other during the night. Where the ground is level, and four to five-inch-diameter straight logs are available, they may be staked at each end to keep them from rolling, and the bed unrolled along them. Another way is to have a cross log at each end, notched to receive the pole ends. After sleeping for a few nights on the bed, it may develop a sag. Then you simply turn it over and sleep on the other side.

Occasional turning keeps the willows straight. Although one may sleep on the bed with nothing more underneath than a couple of blankets or a sleeping bag, it should be remembered that the Indian covered his bed with a buffalo robe. I have used a mattress bag partly filled with dry leaves, preferably those of American beech. Why beech? Because the leaves are especially springy. European peasants for centuries slept on the dry leaves of their native beech in preference to straw, which became musty. In the Ohio Valley, the pioneers continued this custom of stuffing mattresses with beech leaves.

The adaptation described and shown is from Mason's Woodcraft and Camping.[2] The actual Indian bed required about twice as many rods, all whittled flat on the sides so that they fit tightly together. And the Indians didn't use double strings—an additional safety device. It took a long time to make such a bed, but time was of no importance when the finished product lasted for many years. The spiral binding through the holes in the rod ends shows the inventiveness of the originator. If secured with only a loop, the rods would roll around when the bed is reversed, and the sag would still be there.

Many tribes just slept on buffalo robes, and used only the backrest, which was much higher than the one shown. According to the Southwest Museum in Los Angeles, tribes using the complete willow bed included the Arapaho, Blackfoot, Teton Sioux, Cheyenne, and Comanche.

THE AMERINDIAN TIPI AND WILLOW BED

1. Page 13—Reginald and Gladys Laubin, *The Indian Tipi.* Norman, OK: University of Oklahoma Press, 1977.
2. Page 16—Bernard Sterling Mason, *Woodcraft and Camping.* New York: Dover, 1974.

Fig. 5: Plains Indians' willow bed. 1) Bed unrolled and stretched. 2) Small cord passes through holes in rod ends and spirals around large cord. 3) Detail of double cords.

A
DRINK
OF WATER

World War II, Harvard University developed for the Armed Services a superior method of purification using iodine. For use in the field, get an ordinary one-ounce glass medicine bottle with a leakproof plastic cap. Add four to eight grams of USP-grade iodine crystals. Nearly fill the bottle with water, cap it, and shake vigorously for about one minute. Let stand for several minutes while the iodine crystals sink to the bottom. You use the nearly saturated solution above the crystals, *not* the crystals themselves! For water temperatures between 68° and 77° F. add five capfuls (12.5 cc.) of the solution to a quart of water and let stand for 15 minutes. If you have the time, one-half the amount of iodine solution added to the water with a standing time of 40 minutes will improve the taste. Repeat the process each time more sterile water is needed.

Water temperature affects solubility, and hence the saturation point, of the iodine crystals. At 37° F. you need 20 cc. (eight capfuls), but at 104° F. only 10 cc. (four capfuls) are needed. By filling the bottle with water after each withdrawal, you can purify nearly 1,000 quarts before the iodine is entirely dissolved.

Do not use aluminum canteens for water purified by iodine crystals. The iodine can react with the aluminum to poison the water. Plastic canteens are best.

The purity of a woodsman's water supply is of paramount importance. Today it's best to presume that nearly every river, brook, and lake, even in the backcountry, is more or less polluted.[1] The basic method of water purification is boiling. After one minute, most infectious organisms are killed, but not hepatitis viruses, and some nasty organisms that may infect you often remain after such a short boil. Boiling for 20 minutes kills all. If you are cooking over a wood fire, this is practical, but if you are backpacking and are dependent on a little stove, the extra time and fuel needed may call for using a chemical method.

Halazone tablets that liberate chlorine when dissolved in water have been used for many years, but they have several serious disadvantages. During

A DRINK OF WATER
1. Page 18—Excellent methods of water purification are given by James A. Wilkerson, *Medicine for Mountaineering.* Seattle: The Mountaineers, 1975. Also see Kahn and Vischer, Backpacker Magazine 26, May-June 1978; and Backpacker 28. But boiling is still the best method.

BOOTS
AND
CLOTHING
FOR
THE WOODS[1]

Boots[2]

Boots should be as light as possible, but give adequate support and wear. An extra pound on the feet is said to add about five pounds of stress on the back, some say 10. Of course, your weight, that of your pack, if any, and the kind of country you'll be hiking dictate the choice of a boot. For someone weighing up to 160 pounds with a 30-pound pack (or a 180-pound person with no pack), three pounds of boots should be enough. The heaviest pair I've seen in a catalog weighs six pounds six ounces, suitable for a big man with pack, the total weighing perhaps 300 pounds![3]

The catalogs are full of heavy, stiff-soled alpine boots never intended for ordinary trail walking, or for going crosscountry through the forest where the yielding litter-duff-humus layer cushions the feet.

Along woodland trails, alpine boots often hurt the feet. A trail shoe must have a somewhat flexible sole for comfort. Some three-fourths of all those who take to the woods are overshod. A beginner might well choose the best grade of work shoe with a smooth but nonslip sole. Most people may never need anything heavier than three pounds for the pair.

Now then, do you wear boots with lug soles —are you a "waffle-stomper"? What a name for an environmentalist! Until several decades ago, I never saw the tracks (they're more than footprints) of these soles on the soft wilderness trails of the Northeast. Now they're everywhere. Pick up a few sporting goods catalogs, thumb through their pages, and you'll see why. These waffle soles are now the "in thing," and most young hikers don't feel properly shod without them. Ridiculous.

I've never met or corresponded with woodsmen who didn't admit that lug soles cause more damage than plain nonslip soles. The only question is how much more, and this depends upon several things—the kind of soil, the slope, how wet it is, and other factors. Take a look at Fig. 6. I'm not too concerned with boots' effect in mud on level ground, but I *am* concerned with what happens when you climb slopes on sandy loam soils. As you push away with the ball of your foot, the blocks in the pattern you've just stomped into the trail break down. Even if they don't, this pattern is more easily eroded by running water than that from a nonlugged sole.

I built an open box with the top side edges 20° from the horizontal, and packed it firmly with sandy loam soil. I then made two boot impressions, trying to put all my weight each time on the experimental "trail" surface—one with a boot with a plain sole, the other with a lug-soled boot. I then left all to nature. It rained steadily all night. Next morning the rain gauge showed half an inch of precipitation. Repeating the experiment, I got about the same effect from three-eighths of an inch of rain after a 30-minute "pourdown." There now was a striking difference in the appearance of the two tracks. Although both showed slight sheet erosion, the plain-sole impression looked about as it had before the rain. The lug-sole print no longer showed the raised blocks. They were all washed away!

I made another lug-sole track and then, using a thin-bladed spatula, sliced off the raised sand blocks, dried them thoroughly in the sun, and weighed the residue. I got very close to one ounce in weight. On easily eroded soil, assuming about 2½ feet between lugged tracks, one hiker in travelling one mile will have disturbed about 120 pounds of earth!

Not for a moment would I argue that this is a typical case. There are too many variables including slope, numbers of hikers, kind of soil, and moisture content. My only firm belief is that lug soles do indeed promote more erosion than do plain ones or those with a reasonable nonslip tread. Why not try Vibram's Silvato sole with ⅛-inch indentations (No. 4). Presently, Norm Thompson of Portland, Oregon, and L.L. Bean are the only outfitters I know who have boots with this environmentally good sole.[4]

Why are lugs so highly recommended for general use? Safety, say their defenders. Without them, you'll have many a fall.[5] Is this true? All I can say is that in over 30 years, in which I conducted some 3,000 forestry students and others over rough terrain, I never called off a field trip because of the weather, and no one was ever injured by a bad fall. We didn't have lug soles—they weren't around yet. I've safely explored some of the wildest sections of the Adirondacks, including the high peaks, climbed lower trailless rocky slopes of the Wyoming Tetons, traversed part of the immense talus slope at Lake Louise, Banff National Park, Alberta, Canada, and am not unfamilar with the magnificent Sierra Nevada—John Muir's great "Range of Light."

I must conclude that the safety advantage of lug soles is overrated. How much, I don't know. It's in part a subjective thing for you to decide. But millions of day-hikers and backpackers wear lugs in country where they contribute little if any to the hiker's safety—while at the same time clawing at the trails and smashing vegetation.

Smooth neoprene or leather soles can be slippery and dangerous. My favorite shoe was ankle high (six-inch), with a modified moccasin toe and "Cat's Paw" composition sole that clung to smooth rock surfaces very well. My contemporary Bob Marshall, while a student at our Forestry Camp ('24), wore the Munson last Army Shoe; years later in Alaska he appeared to be wearing the same kind of shoe after returning from a 50-day trip in the wilderness. I often wonder what he would have thought of the current millions of waffle-stompers.

Presently, I have a pair of work shoes with cork composition soles. It's no trouble to walk up or down a 30-degree slope on smooth rock surfaces. Crepe or other soles that are not deeply indented are also acceptable. Such shoes are for summer hiking, when snow or ice is no problem. For early spring or autumn in the woods, the leather-topped rubber-footed shoe pioneered by L.L. Bean has served me well and is most comfortable; with 10-inch tops, a pair weighs only two pounds 15 ounces.

L.L. Bean, of Freeport, Maine, an ardent hunter and fisherman, used to suffer from cold, wet feet when hunting in the autumn woods. Like everyone else, he wore all-leather boots. One fall (1912), he had an idea that he thought might do away with all this discomfort. He cut the tops off an old pair of leather boots and had new heavy-duty rubbers sewn to them. He put on two pairs of wool socks, slipped his feet into the new hybrids, and went hunting. Wonderful! His feet stayed dry and warm, and traction was greatly improved. And so was born the prototype of the world-famous Bean hunting shoe. Mr. Bean designed the new rugged but lightweight shoes using the finest leather, specially molded rubber feet with a nonslip chain-pattern tread, and a steel-arch cushioned inner sole. Years later the excellent triangular heel insert was incorporated to eliminate the vertical seam that pressed against the Achilles tendon. In cold, wet woods and in the snow, one could not wish for better footgear.

Two warnings about seemingly unimportant but potentially lethal hazards. The catalog pictures show boot laces tied with the city man's usual bow knot. When traveling in the brush, these loops are a nuisance, apt to snag on some projection, and may give you a bad fall. Lace them so that after tying a square knot (not too tightly), one end will be about three inches long. Cut the long end to match. If the lace is nylon, flame the cut end to harden it. Personally, I prefer rawhide, but not from soon-worn-out pigskin. Get well-tanned cowhide (belt-lacing grade). The other item is hooks, or rings riveted to the outside of the boot. These also can snag or get choked with trash. I prefer plain eyelets.

Naturally the fit and care of your boots are of the greatest importance.[6] Two basics are 1) no slippage or very little at the heel (it causes blisters), and 2) plenty of room for the toes to spread out. Between the boots and your feet should always be wool socks. Wool cushions the feet and absorbs sweat, passing it on to the outermost layers away from the skin. People who think they're allergic to wool may have used too coarse a weave. Nylon can be worn next to the skin. If you wear a thin pair of cotton socks under wool, however, your feet will be damp. Cotton retains moisture. This may not matter in summer. But in winter or at high elevations at any time where frostbite may occur, you'll be in danger.[7]

Wrinkles in socks must be avoided. They promote blisters. Modern stretch socks seem to have solved this problem for some users. Socks come in various lengths. Those that come two or three inches above the boot top may suit you in warm weather, except when hordes of blackflies are on the rampage. Then and in cold weather, wear the longer, calf-length socks.

Clothing

The present generation of woodland hikers may think that blue jeans (the "uniform of youth") are the thing to wear. I have no illusions that I can change this attitude. I can only point out their disadvantages in the woods. 1) Most of them are too tight, evidently to show one's form, rather than for comfort; 2) made of cotton, suitable for dry weather, they are the devil when soaking wet and clammy against your legs. Especially when a strong wind is blowing, they may contribute to hypothermia (see page 96); 3) the blue color attracts mosquitoes.

Again it's WOOL (at least 80 percent if combined with synthetics) for all seasons. For warm weather, the fabric is relatively thin, with a strong hard weave. The pants should be styled generously

enough so that as you walk or climb, there is no binding at the knees, the crotch, or anywhere else. If you want to carry a pair of shorts for open going, fine. I recently came upon a young man clad only in tight shorts climbing the Adirondack Mt. Marcy Trail. The rest of his lily-white body was exposed to a score of circling blackflies which luckily were not in a feeding mood. Someone said, "Look at the blackfly bait." He grinned, "I know it, and if they start to dive-bomb my eyes, I'll run all the way back to the trail-head." Ah, youth!

Back to pants: never woods-walk with cuffs. Pants should reach about an inch below the boot tops. You may want to cut a fringe around the edges. After much woods-walking, you'll have tassels. The fringe promotes faster drying, and some lumberjacks think it gives safety. If the pant snags, one or two of the tassels will tear out, but you'll keep going. Belt or suspenders? I say both, the first for comfortable snugness, the second to carry the weight. Because we're all different, the fitting of everything from boots to hat is an individual matter. Use your own feelings and judgment.

Of course, your shirts as well as your pants should be wool or a mixture of fibers with wool predominating. Two thin shirts worn together are warmer than one thick one, and you have a greater choice of warmth when the temperature changes. If

Fig. 6: Footprints. 1) Plain sole track. 2) Lug sole tracks in mud. 3) Lug pattern torn from trail base is about to crumble or erode. 4) Vibram Silvato sole—indentations are ⅛-inch deep.

even one is too warm, take it off—unless you're surrounded by a cloud of bugs or under the blazing sun. Extensive and severe sunburn must be avoided at all costs. Sweating is to be avoided when possible. It wastes energy, even though it is a necessary part of body-temperature control. Underneath, when not in fly-time, you may wear the Norwegian fishnet undershirt—a classic invention, cool by itself, warm with a shirt over it because of the extra, dead airspaces between the two.

Many outdoorsmen wear a neckerchief to protect the back of the neck from hot sun or biting insects. It can also be worn as an emergency first-aid sling, and of course as a carrier for small things—nuts, cones, etc.

Last of all, the kind of hat to wear. Here you can get many opinions depending on the climate and local conditions. Most old-timers of the greenwood wear a battered 10-to-20-year-old broad-brimmed (about three-inch) felt hat. They are likely to have a great sentimental attachment to it. It has been a part of their long life in the woods and has served them well. It has kept uncounted deer flies from taking out pieces of their scalp, and it's protected them from wind and weather. A featherweight rain bonnet is a good accessory.

The brim of a hat is a great safety device. Many a time in walking through thick young tree growth, I've stopped instantly—warned by the sound that a twig was about to rake my face or poke me in the eye! In hot weather, it's a great comfort to fill the crown partly with a handful of cool moist sphagnum moss.

If the weather is excessively hot, you need another kind of hat, especially if you're in the sun most of the time. Get a lightweight one, well-ventilated, with a brim to shade the eyes; even a broad-visored cap may do. These suggestions are important because large blood-vessels keep a constant supply of blood going to neck and head regardless of the air temperature. This means that the neck and head radiate more heat than any other comparable part of the body. They must be kept warm in cool or cold weather, and as cool as possible in hot weather. For these and other reasons, it's foolhardy to go bareheaded for long periods under the hot sun. Many people who do eventually develop small growths on the face and neck. A few of these may be malignant and require removal. Ask your dermatologist what causes them. The invariable answer? The sun. Another reason for avoiding exposure to

the sun's full glare—and a reason to avoid its reflection from the water—is those marvelous indispensable organs—the eyes. The retina in each eye contains more than 100 million light receptors, each of which passes a tiny flicker of electricity to the brain for interpretation. Although the eye is a relatively tough organ, it needs protection from glare. The multiplicity of kinds and colors of sunglasses does not make the best selection an easy matter. Consult your ophthalmologist.

We now come to parkas of various sorts, sweaters (wool, of course), jackets, and rain gear. Some 50 years ago, Eddie Bauer pioneered prime goose down as a filling in quilted outdoor garments and sleeping bags.[8] Its great advantages include extreme light weight for the amount of insulation it provides when fully expanded, compressibility into a very small volume for carrying, and its ability to spring back to full thickness when pressure is released. If you've always worn wool, there is another pleasant surprise. Goose-down and comparable-quality duck-down quilted garments have an unbelievable comfort range.[9] I can wear my goose-down jacket open in front at 68°F in the house and be equally comfortable with it zipped up outdoors at 32°F. Different amounts of down filling give different comfort ranges, and people vary in their reactions to heat and cold. A long treatise could be written on how to choose and care for a down garment or sleeping bag.[10]

Unfortunately, down is at its best only when dry. Any amount of wetness greatly reduces its insulating value, and if it is soaked, it is practically useless. If you are caught in a driving rainstorm with no way to keep your down garments from drinking in water, you may be in great danger of hypothermia, especially if there is much wind or the temperature is low. The wet down in a garment or bag at freezing temperatures may become little balls of ice. Paul Petzold gives an excellent account of the comparative advanges of down and of DuPont's Dacron Fiberfill II.[11] Another competitive man-made fiber is Celanese Polar Guard made in a continuous filament. These two fillers, unlike natural fibers or down, do not absorb water. If your garment or bag gets wet, you can squeeze out the water and retain much of its value as insulation. Wet wool also has this advantage. The manmade fiber products are much cheaper than down, but have less loft (thickness) and compressibility, and are heavier. It's a matter of compromise.

Rain gear includes ponchos (much argument here), long plastic raincoats—okay on a good trail, but no good in the brush—and lightweight rain suits (jacket and pants). I have an excellent featherweight jacket of waterproof nylon with a parka hood folded and zipped inside the collar, and with unusually large air vents under the armpits. Whenever you wear a waterproof garment over other clothing, you can expect condensation of your body water vapor as it is prevented from evaporating. When you take off the rain gear, the rest of your clothing will feel damp—no great matter if you're wearing wool which dries quickly—or unless high wind and low temperatures may threaten the onset of hypothermia. Then you better put on all the extra clothing you have!

Wool fabrics are not usually considered water resistent. However, unprocessed wool is permeated with a natural fat called lanolin, which is quite efficient at shedding water. Lanolin is accompanied by one or more substances with an unpleasant odor. Therefore, in processing, the wool fat is removed and refined to remove odor. The purified lanolin can be put back into the wool, which then regains its water-shedding property. Lanolin or oil-treated wool garments may suit your needs.

Two synthetic materials now on the market may have solved this ages-old rain-gear sweating problem. Gore-Tex has some nine billion pores to the square inch. Each pore is 20,000 times *smaller* than a drop of water, but 700 times *larger* than a molecule of water vapor.[12] Bukflex II is a competing material.[13] Both are used in laminates. They're waterproof but allow body water vapor to pass to the outside. Before buying a garment, write both companies for their brochures and samples of the material.[14]

Visual Pollution

At this point, I'd like to throw in a few words about the bright blue, red, dazzling yellow, and orange fabrics used in outdoor clothing, pack bags, and tents. Millions of hikers and backpackers wearing these gaudy colors are turning the wilderness into one vast Coney Island. You look out across a magnificent forested valley. Not a sign of humans anywhere. No? Look again. Over on the far side is a trail, and suddenly you see it—a moving bright red spot followed by another, and then another, four altogether. It looks like a line of red ants marching along single file. Your vision of the vast wilderness is ruined. Had these hikers been wearing forest green, brown, or russet clothes and packs, they would never have been seen at that distance. When you enter an established campsite, what do you find? Maybe dozens of tents so brightly colored that they practically knock your eye out. This colorful practice is a relatively recent phenomenon. The old idea was to wear colors and live in tents that blended and harmonized with the greenwood. I don't understand these brightly colored "environmentalists." They must be colorblind!

Of course, during hunting season, a red or blaze-orange jacket and headpiece are essential to protect you from being shot for a deer—even by someone in your own party. The other situation in which color is advantageous is when your group is above timberline and climbing bare rock and snow. You need to be conspicuous both to others in your group and from the air in case help is needed. But even that grand old mountaineer who organized the National Outdoor Leadership School, Paul Petzoldt, writes in his book: "...it is our growing conviction that outdoorsmen should wear greens, browns, and other colors that blend into the environment. Since much of the joy of a wilderness experience lies in not seeing other groups—even at a distance—we feel that inconspicuous tones are to be encouraged."[15] Amen. I've heard it rumored that the British are cracking down on gaudy tents in their campgrounds. If so, bully for them. We should too.

If you are concerned about your visibility when hunting seasons are closed, you might consider carrying a 6 × 6-foot piece of international-orange nylon. In an emergency, you could drape yourself in it or spread it out on the ground where it could be seen from the air.

BOOTS AND CLOTHING FOR THE WOODS

1. Page 19—Adapted from "Stop Walking Away the Wilderness," Backpacker Magazine 22, August 1977.
2. Page 19—For an exhaustive evaluation of boots, see William Kemsley Jr. and the editors of Backpacker Magazine, *Backpacking Equipment Buyer's Guide.* New York: Collier Macmillan, 1977.
3. Page 19—The speed with which "improvements" are being made in equipment of all kinds makes it almost imperative to consult current issues of Backpacker Magazine for new evaluations.
4. Page 20—For an interesting brochure on Vibram's lug soles and other Vibram soles (including the admirable Silvato), write the Quabaug Rubber Company, P.O. Box 155B, North Brookfield, MA 01535. The brochure lists some 40 different tread patterns, three-fourths of which are easy on the trail. Any of them may be applied in place of wornout soles.
5. Page 20—Vibram soles can be bought in the East from Eastern Mountain Sports, 1047 Commonwealth Ave., Boston, MA 02215. In the West: Recreation Equipment, 1525 11th Ave., Seattle, WA 98122.
6. Page 20—For fit and care of boots see Kemsley (1977). Also see Robert S. Wood, *Pleasure Packing.* Berkeley, CA: Condor Books, 1972.
7. Page 21—If you intend to camp in winter, be sure to read Paul Petzoldt, *The Wilderness Handbook.* New York: W.W. Norton, 1974. Petzoldt trained thousands of ski troops during World War II, and he goes into great detail on this important subject.
8. Page 22—Send for the Bauer catalog by writing Eddie Bauer, Third and Virginia, P.O. Box 3700, Seattle, WA 98124.
9. Page 22—For discussion of "goose" vs. "duck" send for the Eastern Mountain Sports catalog, 1041 Commonwealth Ave., Boston, MA 02215.
10. Page 22—To help you choose a down garment or sleeping bag, see Kemsley (1977).
11. Page 22—Petzoldt (1974).
12. Page 23—Gore-Tex Film: W.L. Gore and Associates, Inc., P.O. Box 1220, Route 213 North, Elkton, MD 21921.
13. Page 23—Bukflex II: Peter Storm, 40 Smith St., Norwalk, CT 06851.
14. Page 23—As this book goes to press, an extremely small manmade microfiber called Thinsulate has appeared. It is used as a fill in garments to give nearly twice the insulation of goose down. Write Thinsulate, 223-6SW, 3M Center, St. Paul, MN 55101.
15. Page 23—Petzoldt (1974).

Fig. 7: The blade. 1) Sharpening knife with file. 2) Wire edge and shadow. 3) Tipping blade until shadow disappears. (Newly exposed metal looks shiny but may photograph dark, depending on the angle of illumination.)

THE CAMPER'S TOOLS
Knife, Hatchet, Saw

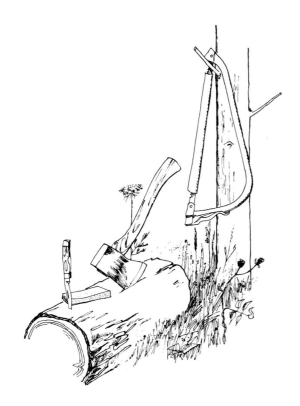

The Knife

"If the iron is blunt, and one does not whet the edge, he must put forth more strength"
Ecclesiastes 10:10

This pithy statement, written more than 2,000 years ago, stands unchallenged for all time. A sharp tool is a joy to use; a dull one is not. Most important, a dull tool is more dangerous. It doesn't "cling" or bite into the wood. It may jump out at you. As "Uncle Dan" Beard used to say, "Knives and hatchets have no brains; they would just as soon cut *you* as anything else." In the many camps I've visited, it's been rare to find a camper's knife that even comes near acceptable sharpness. Usually, I can stare headon at the edge and see that it's so dull it actually has visible width! I'll then (with frozen expression) draw the blade gently and slowly across my throat, to the consternation of the group. Most people don't know what a really sharp edge is, or how to produce one.

I've never yet seen a newly bought jackknife that had a proper edge for whittling. Along the edge of all of them is a very abrupt bevel. This must be widened by sharpening. In the old days one used a large grindstone with a constant water drip. But how many of you have ever seen one? High-speed emery wheels must *never* be used. It's difficult to grind an even bevel, but more important, you can too easily overheat the blade and ruin its temper. Fortunately, a fine file will do the first rough sharpening (Fig. 7, No. 1). Try for a 1/16-inch-wide bevel on a new knife. The one shown has been worn down by many years of whittlin'. The edge is now nearer the thick part of the blade, hence a wider bevel is needed.

A file should always be pushed, never pulled or sawed back and forth. Look at it with your hand lens. Note the "teeth" along each ridge. They point forward, and may be dulled or broken if the file is repeatedly pulled instead of pushed. Use light *diagonal* strokes. Lift the file at the end of each stroke, and every minute or so tap the edge on something solid to clean out the filings.

Hold the knife in one hand, and file in the other; or, if you want more stability, carefully clamp the knife in a suitable vise, and file using both hands. Try to file evenly on both sides of the blade, and watch the newly exposed shiny metal. Very soon, the edge will get so thin that it turns over. Stop filing. You now have the well-known "wire" or "feather" edge (No. 2). You can both see and feel it. The experts say that this should be removed before whetting by drawing the knife blade across a small block of hard wood. I usually don't bother to do it, and I still get a sharp edge.

Whetting stones may be of several materials, artificial or natural. For many years those made of carborundum were most common, but I never really liked them. They always seemed a bit gritty. They do cut fast and will produce a good edge. But I prefer the Ozark Mountains' hard Arkansas stone, which gives a superb edge. Any whetstone needs a lubricant. A light oil is best, but water or saliva will do. The lubricant makes the stone cut faster, and it floats away the tiny particles of metal that otherwise become embedded in the stone and greatly reduce its efficiency.

Now for the essential knack of whetting. Just how to do it is something of a mystery. It's assumed

25

by most outdoor writers that you'll just practice until you get it. On this basis many people waste much time and never do learn how to produce a really sharp edge. Obviously, the very edge of the blade must rest on the stone; but if the blade is tipped up too far, the edge will be dulled rather than sharpened.

Years ago I devised an easy way to ensure that the edge is actually in contact with the stone. It's exact, and anyone can do it. Look at No. 2 and No. 3. Light is shining from the upper left, casting a shadow of the blade upon the stone below. You simply tip the blade until the shadow disappears—no more, no less. "Freeze" your hand in this position, and make from 10 to 20 elliptical passes on the stone, watching to see that you don't unconsciously shift the contact angle. Now turn the blade over and shift your position so that again the light casts the needed shadow. After sharpening both sides, stop and look carefully at the edge, using a hand lens if you have one. Are fragments of the wire edge still there? Probably. Whet both sides again, but use fewer strokes.

When the entire edge looks smooth, test it by whittling a piece of soft wood. Some of us oldsters test the edge on a dry thumb. If the knife is sharp, it sort of clings. We definitely advise you *not* to do this! But if you'd like to try it, it's your thumb, and don't blame us if you get a "leetle" cut. Certainly it's not to be taught to youngsters. After considerable use, the keen edge dulls, and the bevel you filed may darken. Unless the edge is nicked—and to suggest this is an insult to a good craftsman—filing is not in order. Just a touchup with the whetstone will do.

You may want to try another method of whetting: hold the knife in one hand and the stone in the other, and rub the stone along the bevel from one end to the other using a circular motion. There must be a strong light shining on the blade so you can see just what the stone is doing. As you whet, the slightly darkened metal on the bevel surface is ground off, and the shiny "new" metal underneath appears. From this you can gauge the all-important angle of contact between stone and knife.

What sort of knife should you own? For all-around camp use you can't beat the Scout knife, too well-known to illustrate. For many years, I preferred a white handle—easier to spot if it is lost in summer woods and fields. But for winter camping a dark handle is the thing. The Swiss Army knife solves the color problem with its red handle. These knives come with various assortments of tools. The Boy Scout Whittler has blades of carbon steel, a metal long known for its virtue of holding a keen edge. Swiss knife blades are stainless steel. Each has its virtues; I'll not enter the argument. There are too many variables.

Just sittin' and whittlin' on a stick of wood was a universal soul-soothing recreation of early Americans. It didn't matter whether you actually made something. To feel the sharp knife blade slicing along the grain of a piece of old-growth soft pine relaxed your tensions and made you feel good all over. And as the long, curling shavings formed a bunch at the end of the stick, their piney fragrance might tell of many spring and summer growing seasons long before you were born. You could be whittling wood that was formed way up on the swaying trunk, where the rush of clean, music-making wind made every slender pine needle tremble and sing. Every country boy just had to have a good jackknife. Without one, how could he make a bow and arrows, or carve something, or play mumblety-peg, or do all the other things that satisfied his creative urge? Now we give our children expensive toys soon neglected, forgetting that something we make ourselves is more fun and treasured longer. When you buy a knife, avoid a cheap one. The blades will probably be made of a poor grade of steel that won't hold an edge. There are some exceptions, however; buy one and try it before committing yourself to enough for a group.

Opening and closing a knife is second nature to those of us who've used one for a long time. Closing poses the most danger; and as I began to write this section, I observed how I had done it for 60 years and decided it might not be the safest way for beginners! Like many thousands of other whittlers, I have held the open knife pinched between finger tips and thumb, palm down, and pressed the palm of the other hand on the back of the blade to close it. The trouble is you do it blind; the knife is hidden behind your hands. See Fig. 8, No. 1 for a safer way. You can see what you're doing. The end of the handle is firmly anchored in the angle between thumb and forefinger, giving the best leverage. An occasional drop of oil on the hinge makes a new knife easier to open and close.

And so to whittling. It looks deceptively easy. I once handed a stick of soft pine and a sharp knife to my teenage "model" and asked him to whittle a frill stick like that in No. 2. He had difficulty in getting even an occasional shaving to stay on the stick. He just whittled them off—poor coordination! I was amazed. I'd completely forgotten my own similar initial experience when about eight years old.

A basic fact to remember is that any edged tool has a saw blade, no matter how sharp it is. You need only to look at the edge with a microscope to see the teeth. This means that to get the smoothest wood surface possible when whittling, the knife should not be pushed straight ahead—if possible you should use a slight sliding motion. This takes practice. It makes little difference how you whittle a frill stick; but for fine carving, especially on the end grain, the blade must be drawn lengthwise (No. 3). This also gives the smooth surface needed for wood identification with a hand lens. *Keep your thumb below the end of the stick.* My associates and I have said this thousands of times to our students, only to see several of them a few minutes, hours, or days later with their thumbs sticking partway up above the stick end. As the sharp blade is drawn across, it

Fig. 8: Whittling. 1) A safe way to close a knife. 2) Whittling a frill stick. 3) Making a smooth end cut.

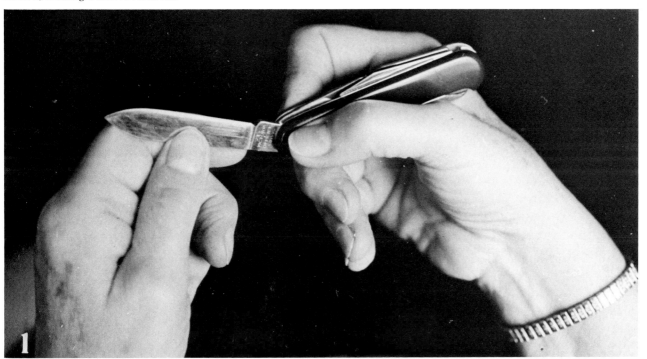

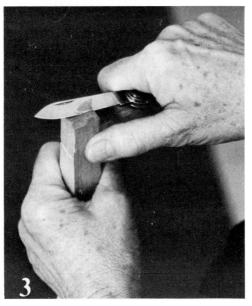

often slips. A thumb is a very poor backstop indeed!

Another hair-raising thing to see is some camper sitting on a log cutting notches in a stick that is resting on his leg just above the knee. Better you should hold the stick on something solid that has no feelings.

And why would you want to cut a lot of notches in a stick? In the Appalachian Mountains, they make an interesting toy called a "whimmy-diddle" stick. They cut a row of notches along a piece or stout twig of hard wood. A small propeller is fitted loosely onto the tip. By rubbing a stick back and forth across the notches, you can make the propeller not only spin but also, if you know the trick, reverse at your command. This is much more than just a simple toy. I first saw one only a few years ago, but long before that, Professor E. F. McCarthy, one-time head of our Silviculture Department, had shown me how to make a more sophisticated model that he called a "Soo-soo" stick. There was a story to go with it. Soo-soo was an old Siwash Indian chief whose spirit inhabited the stick. If he wasn't asleep, and if you called his name in a respectful tone, he would reverse the propeller! You can concoct some infinite variations with this basic story.

I whittled the McCarthy model, Fig. 9, No. 1., from a hickory branchlet ½-inch in diameter and seven inches long. Leave the bark on the handle end, and carefully whittle the rest of the stick so that it has four sides (a square in cross-section). Along each edge, carve small, evenly spaced notches until you near the end, which can be tapered. The carefully drilled hole in the propeller is 1/16-inch in diameter, large enough to give a loose fit on the shaft, which is a common pin pushed into the pith. It's important that the propeller balances. If one side is heavier than the other, carve off a smidgen to attain equal weight on both sides. Rubbing a small (kitchen-match size) stick or a nail back and forth across the notches makes the propeller spin like mad (No. 2).

Anyone can do it. But to make the prop *reverse* is something else again. People watching you get all sorts of ideas on how it's done. The only way consistently to make it reverse with the "Soo-soo" request is to place your thumb and forefinger exactly as shown. When you push with your thumb, the propeller spins one way. Now release the pressure and pull against the stick with your finger. The prop stops and spins the other way. If you are careful how you shift pressure from thumb to finger, no one will

ever discover the reversal secret. Soo-soo is an instant attention-getter for young and old alike. I've had fun asking engineers and physicists to explain how the horizontal vibrations are changed to rotary motions, and why the prop reverses when pressure is shifted from one side of the stick to the other. I'll not spoil your exploration by saying any more.

In cutting down saplings one to two inches in diameter, a useful trick is to bend them sharply at the base. Then saw the knife back and forth across the top of the bend. Only a few strokes are needed, but you may have to finish by bending the sapling or sprout the other way.

I haven't mentioned everything you should know about your knife. There are useful lists in the Scout Handbooks. Never run with an open knife in your hand. Finally, every time you whittle or carve or do anything else with the knife, keep your eye on the blade and ask yourself: if the blade slips, will it slash or stab human flesh? The flesh may be yours or that of someone standing beside you. If the answer is "yes," only a fool would fail to stop and change position to assure safety.

The Hatchet

A hatchet may be defined as a lightweight short-handled axe to be swung primarily with one hand. But you'll find all sorts of weights and handle lengths—a large hatchet is really a small axe. Fig. 10, No. 1 shows a hatchet being used two-handed for chopping out the upper part of the under-cut on a small tree. Two hands give better control than one—especially important to youngsters. Note the kneeling position. Many books show the chopper standing. I too used to chop this way, not realizing the possible danger. Then one day a physical-education senior at Sargent Camp cut her instep slightly. After she was patched up, I asked, "How did it happen?" and she showed me. Very simple: she was new at it. The hatchet just missed the tree, and the next thing in line was her foot. She was lucky it wasn't worse. From then on, we knelt. In that position a missed blow can only end with the blade in the ground. Kneeling also lets you make a much better crosswise cut in the tree.

No. 2 shows that in limbing you must chop toward the top of the tree. This is because of the long, fibrous wood grain running up and down the tree and out toward the branch tips. A blade driven into the crotch from the topside may just stick there, or even split off the branch from the trunk. And *always* keep the trunk between you and the limb you're cutting off. Many a lumberjack too lazy or too confident of his skill to bother with one or both of these rules has seriously cut himself with his axe.

No. 3 depicts Moosewood's "patented" chopping block for severing small stuff. The top is slanted away from the chopper. It could well be slanted even more than shown. A slanted top is safer and more comfortable for the beginner than one that's straight across. The height of the block should be matched to the height of the average user. Notice that the blade cuts diagonally. The wood structure parts easiest this way. Cutting straight across takes more energy. If the blade doesn't go through with the first blow, raise stick and hatchet together and

swing them down again. This is the "contact method." If the stick is crooked, first turn it so there's no space under it where the blade is to strike. Otherwise, it may bounce, and when severed, the end may fly back in your face or sail away to hit someone nearby. When chopping, keep observers 15 feet or more away from you.

I have no use for a hatchet with a metal handle. It feels dead in your hand when you chop. Unlike a wood handle, a metal one lacks springiness, and you get a greater shock to your hand and arm as you use it.

Although a wood handle is best, it has one fault. In dry weather, it may shrink enough so that when you chop, the axe head loosens slightly and

Fig. 9: 1) A "Soo-soo" stick. 2) Spinning the propeller. 3) The proper position for consistent reversal of the propeller on "command."

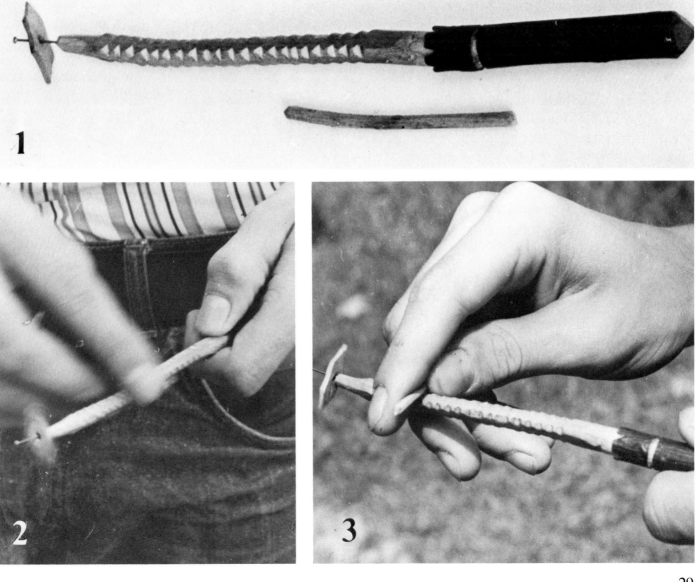

begins to creep off the end of the handle—potentially dangerous. Fig. 11, No. 1 shows how to drive the head back into place. "Common sense" may tell you to reverse the hatchet vertically and drive the head down on the handle. Not so. The head is many times heavier than the handle. The old principle of inertia dictates that you drive the lighter into the heavier.

When the head is seated once more, what then? If the head end of the handle has a patented screw wedge, you just tighten the screw. If not, set the hatchet in a pail of water and leave it there for a couple of hours. The swelling pressure of wood is enormous. If the hatchet is left in water too long, the wood structure may be slightly crushed; then when it dries out, the head may be looser than before. All you can do is experiment and avoid long soaking. If this doesn't work, the old wedge must be drilled out and a new one made. Use a piece of hard wood, as bone-dry as you can get it. Make the new wedge one or two inches longer than seems necessary. It's easier to drive, and the projecting end is then sawed off flush.[1] (For other pointers, such as how to sharpen, see page 34 The Axe.)

Knives and hatchets, especially hatchets, have an irresistible attraction for youngsters and oldsters alike. Just leave one standing against a tree, and in no time at all one of your group will go over, pick it up, and with a glint in his eye look around for something to chop. Knives and hatchets should be considered as personal as a toothbrush. They should not in ordinary circumstances be loaned or borrowed. It's bad woods etiquette to ask someone to let you use his edged tools.

Saws for the Camper

Modern tubular bowsaws are a great improvement over the old-fashioned bucksaw, but for the camper the collapsible Sven Saw is the thing. It weighs only about 14 ounces and easily cuts "timber" up to four or five inches in diameter. The blade should be hinged into its metal back for safe carrying. Carried bare, it's all too easy, as your hand swings forward, for the frame to strike something along the trail. On the rebound, the needle-sharp teeth may rip your clothing or flesh. I have a scar on my knee to prove it!

Fig. 11, No. 3 shows a sawbuck simply made and bound tightly with binder twine. When starting a cut, keep your steadying hand well back from the saw, which may jump out. Use an easy stroke, letting the weight of the saw do the work. Using one of these saws can and should be pure enjoyment. If it isn't, the teeth are dull or not set properly. Note the two kinds of teeth: the pointed *cutting teeth,* and the notched *rakers* that clean out the cut wood (Fig. 18, p. 47). A new blade usually lasts a season or two and can then be replaced with another one for a nominal cost. When sawing resinous or other woods that tend to gum up the blade, squirt a little kerosene along it. Always keep the saw clean and bright, and covered with a film of light oil.

These saws have taken over much of the work formerly done with the hatchet, which now has limited use. When felling saplings, the saw makes a smooth front cut. The hatchet then cuts out a wedge of wood above it, and the saw finishes the job with the back cut. A smooth stump is left. For cutting up firewood to length, the saw produces smooth ends and in general is safer to use. But lots of people like to chop with a hatchet, and who says they don't have the privilege?

Fig. 10: Chopping with a hatchet. 1) Kneeling position for safety. 2) Keeping trunk between chopper and limb. 3) Safety chopping block with slanted top.

THE CAMPER'S TOOLS

1. Page 30—All the labor needed to put a hatchet head back in place may no longer be necessary. Write the Chair-Loc Company, Lakehurst, NJ 08733, for a three-ounce bottle of Chair-Loc (current price: $1.50). This liquid penetrates the wood fibers, causing them to swell permanently. No more loose handles. It works.

Fig. 11: 1) Tightening a loose hatchet handle. 2) Some soaking may keep it tight. 3) Camper's sawbuck, with a Sven saw.

THE WOODSMAN'S TOOLS
Axe, Saw, Peavey

The big-timber woods used to be a pleasant place to visit and work in. The chief man-made sounds were the "thunk" of sharp axes biting into green wood, the rhythmic song of the two-man crosscut saw, and the occasional crash of a falling forest giant. The first two sounds are almost gone forever, replaced by the snarl and stink of the efficient chain saw. (In some places the deer recognize this new sound as a "dinner bell" and come from a long way off to browse on the tops of the fallen hardwood trees.) One logger can now cut several times as much wood as two men could with a crosscut saw. However, for safety and for other reasons, two men may still work together when felling, limbing, and bucking forest trees.

Although the axe and crosscut saw seem to be antiques, they are still very much a part of the American scene. At hundreds of annual woodsmen's field days, chopping and sawing contests keep alive the ancient skills.

The Axe

The lore of the axe is deeply embedded in our early history and language. "Don't fly off the handle" came from the danger of using an axe with a loose head. "Hew to the line and let the chips fall where they may" referred to hewing out, with a special broad-axe, square timbers from round logs. "He's a chip off the old block" needs no comment. And of course there was the Great Railsplitter, Abraham Lincoln.[1]

The origin of the axe is extremely ancient. You may recall how Ulysses, after many hair-raising adventures on the way home from Troy, was caught in a terrible storm. His ship was wrecked, his entire crew drowned, and he himself, more dead than alive, was thrown up on the beach of the goddess Calypso's island. She took a fancy to him, and he lived with her for several years. But then he became overwhelmed with homesickness and spent his days sitting on the beach, gazing out to sea, the salt tears coursing down his cheeks. When the beautiful Calypso saw that she could no longer charm him, she gave him a great bronze axe sharpened on both sides (double-bitted), with a beautiful olive-wood handle. With this he cut down the tall "sky-stretching" pines and built his escape raft.

The double-bitted axe was in use at least a thousand years before the Odyssey was written (circa 1000 B.C.). With a short handle, it was used as a weapon in war, and as a tool in sacrifices.

For many of us, the double-bitted axe will always be our favorite. It has superb balance when you swing it. You can sharpen one bit to a super-keen edge for fine chopping, and leave the other with a more abrupt bevel for limbing or splitting. Of course, you must be very careful in handling it because, as Paul Bunyan used to say, it cuts "both coming and going." When not in actual use, it must be muzzled. If you don't have a good heavy leather sheath, cut two lengths of slit garden hose, fit one over each blade, and hold them in place with several heavy rubber bands. For general use, the double-bit is not a recommended camp axe.

The axe most of you have seen if not used is the poll axe (Fig. 12). Poll means head, as in poll tax, meaning head tax. A poll axe is also called a single-

Fig. 12: The axe. 1) Line of sight along the edge must coincide with the center line of the helve. 2) Wide growth rings indicate strength. 3) Medium-weight poll axe. 4) Filing. 5) Whetting.

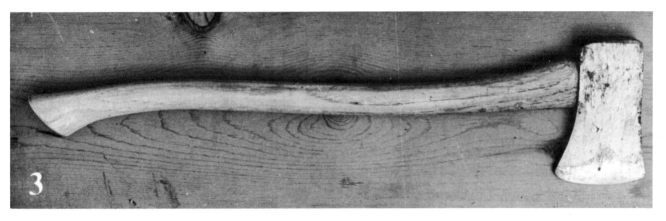

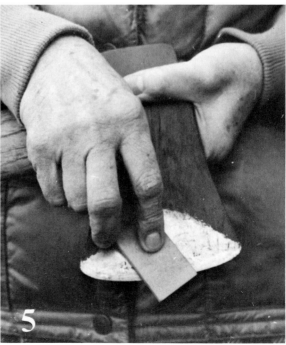

bitted axe. A man's axe has a 3½-to-4-pound head and a 32-to-36-inch hickory handle (helve). For most camp use, a boy's axe is the thing, with a 2½-pound head and a 26-inch helve. There are several head shapes besides the one shown. A favorite of many woodsmen is the tomahawk-shaped Hudson's Bay model.

If possible, buy your axe personally so you can sight along its helve (Fig. 12, No. 1) to see that it's perfectly straight; a helve with a sidewise curve is no good. While your eye checks straightness, also see that the edge of the blade lines up perfectly with the center line of the helve. If there's divergence, reject the axe. Finally, look at the growth rings on the end of the sloping "lamb's foot" (No. 2). The wider the rings the better (see p. 52). For best strength, they shouldn't be much less than one-eighth of an inch wide. Now run your hand up and down along the helve. It should feel glass-smooth. It probably isn't. Sand it down, finishing with the finest-grit sandpaper you can buy. Old-timers did an excellent job by carefully scraping with pieces of broken window glass.

Look at No. 3. The slanting end of the lamb's foot is just for looks. Measure back about an inch, and with a fine-tooth saw cut off the end so that the surface is at a right angle to the helve. Now if the axe head loosens, there is a square end to use in driving the helve back into place.

If the axe is for splitting only, the blade needs little if any thinning. Just a touchup along the edge with a file will do. But if you want to learn how to chop, some time must be spent in thinning the blade (No. 4). Nothing surpasses the old-fashioned wet grindstone if you can find one. The file shown is an 8-inch mill-bastard. (Why "bastard"? Because the rows of teeth per inch on the flat sides are not the same as those on the file edges.) I'm sure the "experts" won't like my diagonal file strokes. Theoretically, the grooves should be at right angles to the blade. In practice, their direction makes little difference, especially after the blade is whetted or honed.

A file can be treacherous. It may slip suddenly. If you're filing straight toward the edge, you could cut a finger. If you still prefer this method, make a file guard from two small pieces of wood. Drill the ends for small bolts that will clamp the guard firmly at the base of the file.

As you file, the shiny exposed steel should approximate a fan-shaped pattern. The surface

should not be flat right down to the edge. File so that there is a smooth, slightly rounded bevel along the edge. A perfectly flat surface on both sides of the blade would promote its sticking in the log you chop. The rough (feather) edge finally produced should be carefully whetted off by stroking with the file on alternating sides (No. 5). Watch carefully and be sure that the hone is at the proper vertical angle. As the feather edge disappears, look along the blade with your hand lens. The edge should look smooth. A sharp axe can whittle just as good a frill stick as a sharp knife.

Such an edge must be guarded at all times when not in use. Sheath it at once when you're through chopping. Don't leave an axe sticking in a stump or log as shown in many books. It's too easy to trip over the helve, especially at night. Also, in certain trees, moisture and chemicals may stain the blade and cause it to rust. One day at Sargent Camp, a senior girl had just finished grinding and whetting a fine edge on her axe. Not wanting to use it right then, she drove the blade into the ground. You could hear the grating sound of steel against New England sand and gravel.

I said to her in amazement, "Why did you do that?"

Equally amazed, she replied, "Because that's the way mah daddy taught me."

I asked, "Where do you live?"

The answer: "In Mississippi, along the river."

I should have known. Over thousands of acres there you couldn't find a stone or even a speck of sharp sand—nothing but unending fine soft alluvium. Perhaps down there, from the safety angle, what she did made sense. But to keep an axe from rusting, it must stay dry and, preferably, kept oiled when not in use.

Did you ever see someone pick up an axe by the end of its helve and start to walk along with the head dangling dangerously close to his feet? *Always grasp the helve right behind the head with the blade slanting down diagonally away from you.* How do you hand an axe to someone? Do you hold the head in your hand and extend the helve horizontally so he can grasp its end? Such politeness could be manslaughter. The novice doesn't know that as you let go, the head may swing down right into his foot. It takes a strong man to hold an axe straight out by its helve end. To pass an axe, hold it vertically with your hand about a foot behind its head, the blade to

Fig. 13: Chopping with an axe. 1) Learner's safety rig. 2) A possible disaster. 3) Proper position: back and knees bent, helve nearly horizontal at the end of the stroke.

one side. Then he has a choice of just where he wants to take hold of the handle.

Teaching axemanship to novices can be a hair-raising experience. It's the duty of the instructor to see that there is never a cut foot or leg. Years ago, at the Sargent College Camp, Moosewood dreamed up a safety chopping rig (Fig. 13, No. 1) that protected several hundred physical education seniors over a period of seven years. Not one of them was ever clumsy enough to swing the axe over the top of the securely staked 2 × 6-inch plank! I had intended to go no further than the proper use of the hatchet, but one day old Dean Hermann presented me with five just-bought axes and said "Here, teach the girls how to chop vood!"

Axemanship instruction should really be a one-to-one thing, but if you set up three of these rigs safely spaced in the open, you can watch fairly well what's happening. (Just be sure there are no overhead obstructions of any kind that might deflect the axe. An unnoticed backyard clothesline has been known to snag an axe and bounce it right back at the chopper!) We had lots of white pines that needed thinning, so we had plenty of green 7-to-8-inch logs for practice chopping. Any soft wood with few knots is excellent (soft pine, spruce, basswood, poplar). Avoid hemlock with its glass-hard knots, and hardwoods in general. Such hardwoods as hickory, beech, and oak are not fun to chop.

The experienced chopper stands on top of a log, makes a 45° notch on one side, turns around, does the same on the other side, and then steps off as his last skillful blow severs the log. To approximate this method notice again No. 1; the backstop touches the log, which is firmly bedded into two notched cross-logs that keep it off the ground. The log being chopped must feel firm when struck with the axe. The chopper stands as near as possible to the backstop. If he doesn't, the helve may strike the plank, doing the helve no good.

You can tell a skillful axeman by the size of his chips. The fewer and larger they are, the better he is.

You can chop a series of notches all along the log, shifting it as necessary. Do you have a treehouse, or a tree that would be great for climbing except that the first branch is 10 to 15 feet above the ground? One of these notched logs, the top firmly anchored in the first fork, makes a good ladder exactly the same as those made by primitive man for thousands of years. To make the chopping log do

double duty, you simply roll it over and make a series of notches on the other side. The dried chips and split sections make good kindling.

The chopper shown is right-handed. To make the forehand stroke, his left hand should grasp the helve an inch or two above the lamb's foot. His right hand encircles the helve about a quarter of the way down from the axe head. Starting with the axe horizontal, he swings it up along his right side and over his right shoulder. Then he eyes his target spot and brings the axe down, the right hand sliding swiftly so that as the blade bites into the log, the top hand meets the lower one as shown. An axe is not a baseball bat and shouldn't feel like one as you bring it down. The feeling is more like that of throwing the head at the target spot. Do not force the axe. Let the weight of the head do the work. Take it easy. Speed chopping is only for those who've practiced for a long time. Accuracy is your goal. You're not much of a chopper until you can hit precisely along the line your eye chooses—not once but time after time. When you finally can do it, you'll get a feeling of joyous competence that lasts a lifetime.

Before even finishing this story of notching, I must introduce Peter McLaren (Fig. 14), the world's champion axeman from 1906 to 1950, when he retired at age 68. An Australian, he travelled to many lands where local champions were eager to challenge him. For a long time, he took part in nearly 500 contests a year, and finally got so good at it that he gave all challengers a 50-percent time bonus! With that, he was defeated only three times—never in the U.S. It was my privilege to see him in action near the end of his career. He was only of moderate height, but powerfully built, and none of us at our annual forestry field day had ever seen such speed and accuracy with an axe.

He told us: "Never drive all of the blade into uncut wood—the axe may stick. The first blow is near the *top* of the log with a bit of the blade showing above. The second is near the *bottom* with a little of the blade in the clear below. The third cut in the *middle* exactly connects the first two. As you make this third blow, you give the axe a little twist to loosen the chip. Now you shift your body for the backhand stroke and chop the other side of the notch—high, low, middle."

You can see how he did it. On the sixth blow on an uncut log, the twist threw out an enormous chunk of wood. Six more cuts, and he'd made a perfect notch with smooth sides right to the log's center.

Turning quickly, he did the same on the other side, and as the last blow landed, the log parted. He could chop a log in two in less time than it's taken me to tell about it. His record on a 20-inch-diameter log was two minutes, 12 seconds.

After a while, the beginner may decide he no longer needs the safety chopping rig (Fig. 13, No. 1). Without it, his stance must change. You've probably already noticed No. 2 and No. 3. Study them carefully. You can't safely stand up close to the log, because if you do happen to miss, there's nothing but thin air to stop the blade from slashing down into you. Many even tolerably good axemen have been seriously injured in this way.

Years ago Prof. E. F. McCarthy, a fine woodsman as well as a professional forester at our college, said, "When you chop, stand well back, bend your back and knees, and swing the axe so that when the blade strikes the log, the helve is horizontal. This way, you'll never cut yourself." He and I taught thousands of people of all ages how to chop safely using his method. It may be that you want to cut the log in two. If so, you'll just have to roll it over and chop through from the other side.

Although I don't believe that speed chopping events have a place in children's camps, there are

Fig. 14: Peter McLaren demonstrates professional chopping. (Photos by Ames Inc.)

Take a firm stance on the log and grip the axe as shown.

Position of hands and axe at top of stroke. Note that the head is down —eyes on the cut.

Hands are together at completion of stroke. Note that axe strikes upper side of log.

Second stroke should place the axe in the lower side of log as shown.

Third stroke places the axe in the middle of log and throws out the chip.

Top position for Backhand Stroke, bringing axe into line with other face of V-shaped cut.

39

several things to learn from Fig. 15, No. 1. Here is a competitor chopping against time at one of the annual field days at SUNY College of Environmental Science and Forestry.[2] Most important are the metal foot and leg guards. The squared log gives a better foothold than a round one. Note the triangular frames spiked into each end. This right-handed chopper has shifted his body to make the backhand strokes. See how few chips there are, and their large size.

Splitting wood with an axe will be more important to you than chopping, so why didn't I start with it? Because it can be dangerous for beginners who've never used an axe. To split safely, you should be able to land a blow within one-eighth of an inch of where you aimed. Also, splitting raises all sorts of problems that don't exist with simple chopping. Back in the days when most people lived on farms or in small towns, youngsters watched their fathers split wood for the stoves that cooked their food the year round and heated their homes in winter. With a farm woodlot, they were completely independent and had no worries about an energy crisis. As soon as they were able, the kids had the job of keeping the home woodboxes full—a never-ending chore.

At Dr. Sharp's National Camp, I was responsible for axe instruction. Among our Teachers College students was a young man born and raised on a farm. He convinced me that he was completely at home with an axe and had been splitting stove wood for 10 years. So in advance of any instruction I let him have an axe. That very first evening he was splitting a billet and suddenly slashed his foot. That was the end of his two-week outdoor education. He was hospitalized, and I never forgave myself for not watching him split before issuing the axe. And what had he done wrong? Something thousands of farm boys learned to do. He had a pile of sawed small-log pieces perhaps 16 inches long that would burn better if split down the middle. He stood one of them on end, slanting steeply against a log lying on the ground. Then, as he'd done many times before, he put the toe of his shoe against the lower end of the billet to anchor it while he hit the top with the axe!

You may think this is suicidal, but it's not necessarily so. The trick is to give the axe a slight twist just as the blade goes into the wood, or to bring the axe down so that the blade is slightly angled from the vertical as the edge strikes the top of the piece. This technique not only gives greater splitting leverage but also, and most important, the downward momentum of the axe head is killed, or nearly so. But something went wrong. The piece split too easily, and the blade rushed down into his foot.

Putting your toe against the piece is always hazardous because there are so many variables: softness or hardness of the kind of wood, moisture content, rate of growth, presence of knots. Never allow campers or students to split in this way.

No. 3 shows the usual way of splitting firewood—on a chopping block, the larger in diameter the better. When splitting, you can bring the axe straight up on the backswing instead of over the shoulder as in chopping. The hands can be closer together at the beginning of the downward stroke. For safety, don't forget that at the end of the swing the helve must be horizontal or nearly so. If the piece doesn't split with the first blow and is still clasping the blade, raise axe and piece together and swing them down onto the chopping block—the "contact method" again. If you're a husky teenager or adult and have much heavy splitting to do, you can graduate to a man's axe (3½-to-4-pound head). With its longer helve, it packs much more of a wallop than the boy's axe.

If you look at the end of a drying log section, you can see scores of tiny radial cracks running from the outside toward the center. These are usually along the wood rays, ribbonlike bands with relatively thin, weak cell walls. Stresses in wood from drying are enormous. Wood shrinks about twice as much tangentially as it does radially, so radial cracks develop. It makes sense to take advantage of these cracks when you split wood.

On a small-diameter piece, aim to hit it through the center. If the diameter is twice the length of the axe blade, the first blow should make a radial cut from the near side to the center. A crack from top to bottom may or may not open up. Either way, the blade often sticks. Don't wrestle with the axe to get it out. Smack down on the end of the helve with the palm of your hand. This should free the blade. Repeat if necessary. Don't put your free hand on top of the piece near the embedded blade and try to yank it out. It just might jump out and bite you. If the axe still sticks after several smacks on the helve end, put the log section horizontally on the ground and work the axe back and forth until it's free. Most of the time, this isn't necessary.

With the billet back on the chopping block, your second blow should place the blade in line with

40

Fig. 15: Chopping. 1) Woodsman's field-day chopping rig. Note foot and shin metal safety guards. 2) For learners, hands kept low at the end of the stroke, safety log in front. 3) Splitting on a chopping block. Helve is kept horizontal.

the first cut, and extending from the center to the far side. If you're lucky, the piece splits; if not, one more blow in the center should do it. You can then split each half in two, and reduce the quarters to smaller sizes. In doing so, you can also split at right angles to the radial cracks unless you hit a knot. A knot is just an embedded branch that got covered by new wood as the trunk grew. You won't have much luck chopping a knot crosswise. Wood being split is often full of "gremlins." As L. B. Sharp used to say with a twinkle in his eye, "Splitting wood, and doing some other things in camp, take years and years of experience!"

If you have some half-round split pieces of wood, there's a beginners' rig (No. 2) that's safer than the chopping block. The flat side of the piece rests solidly on the flattened surface of a log as shown. The safety log in front protects the axeman's feet. Be sure the end of the piece doesn't stick out over the side of the supporting log. This rig is good for small stuff or short pieces of plank that will lie flat.

For the beginner especially, it's much easier and safer to split a large-diameter log section with a light (eight-pound) sledgehammer and steel wedges than it is to whale away at it with an axe. Fig. 16, No. 1 shows the way it's done. The outside wedge is driven in first. Pretty soon it may get too difficult to drive it further. A radial crack has probably started toward the center and down the side. Drive the second wedge into this crack. Before long, the outer one should loosen. Drive it in some more, and then alternate your blows until the piece pops in two. A third wedge is good insurance in the unusual case when both wedges get stuck.

Take easy strokes, letting the weight of the hammer do the work. Watch out for a loose wedge falling out. It weighs about four pounds and could easily smash a toe or two if you don't keep your feet in the clear. Do not drive both wedges in tightly their full length unless it's obvious that the chunk is about to split. Try to ensure that one wedge is always loose enough to be knocked out easily. There are a few woods with interlocked grain that are difficult or almost impossible to split. These include elms, black gum, and sycamore.

Never use an axe as a wedge or as a sledgehammer to drive a steel wedge (No. 2). The steel in an axe head is soft, except for the blade, which is highly tempered to hold an edge. I've visited many a camp where axes had been misused in this way. The

sides of the eye begin to spread, the helve loosens, and the axe is ruined. The only use for such an axe is to drive it temporarily into a stump where it makes a dandy anvil (if you need one).[3]

No. 3 shows how to split soft woods with wedges of hardwoods such as hickory, beech, oak, or hophornbeam (ironwood). Saw a straight piece two or three feet long, slant it on the chopping block, and, with a hatchet, strike straight down, first on one side and then the other, to make the wedge. Then saw off the excess top and repeat the process. You can use an axe, held close behind its head (choked up short), but be sure you keep track of what's happening to the other end of that long helve. If your short swing is too radial instead of straight down, the helve end may bump into something, including the chopping block, and deflect the blade at you. Hardwood wedges can, of course, be driven with hatchet, axe, or wooden club.

Tree felling, a hard-hat job, is also a high art, and to get experience you should practice with saplings not more than four inches in diameter. It's assumed that you are on your own land. *If not, you must get the owner's definite permission.* Further, he should go with you to the area and mark the trees he'd like removed. These will be shaded dying ones, cripples, diseased trees, those too close together for good growth, and inferior species (such as an ironwood crowding a fine straight white ash or basswood).

First, decide which way you'd like the tree to fall. It must have enough clear space so it won't snag or hang up in another tree on the way down. In most cases, don't try to fell a tree against its natural lean, or against a strong wind. Look up into the crown branches. Are those on one side of the tree much longer and heavier than those on the other? Other things being equal (which they usually aren't), the tree will fall toward the heavier side. While you're looking up, are there any broken dead branches that just "hang by a hair"? If so, walk away and choose another tree unless you can first dislodge those "widow makers" so that they fall to the ground. Dead trees are usually more dangerous to fell than live ones, and if a dead tree is also badly decayed, leave it alone; it may have nesting holes that woodpeckers have laboriously chipped out. The trunk is of no use to you anyway.

Once you've decided where to fell your tree, lay a few cross-logs at right angles along its path. This will keep the fallen trunk off the ground. Later when you saw it into lengths, your sharp saw teeth won't be dulled by running into the dirt.

Kneel at the base of the tree, and with your bowsaw or Sven saw make the horizontal *undercut* one-fourth or one-third of the way through the tree's diameter. If the tree has a butt swell, the cut is usually made just above it. This undercut aims the tree in the direction it should fall and is of course at a right angle to it. Then chop out a wedge of wood above (a 45° cut). Before using a hatchet or axe for any purpose, look around and up to see if bushes or tree limbs are in the way of your swing. Even small branches in the axe's course can alter the swing dangerously.

With the undercut made, the *back cut* on the other side of the tree is started about two inches above the sawed base of the undercut. The back cut

Fig. 16: Wedges. 1) Large log sections split with sledgehammer and steel wedges. 2) Axe ruined by repeatedly striking it with another axe. 3) Wedges of a hard wood used to split a softer wood.

must parallel the undercut. Keep checking to see that it does. If you "cut the corner"—that is, your saw runs into the undercut on one side while there's still some uncut wood on the other—the tree will fall toward that side and not exactly where you had planned. If necessary at this point, clear an escape path 15 feet or so to one side and a little behind the probable path of the falling tree.

Never stand behind the butt. In falling, the tree may strike another tree, and the butt will shoot back like a battering ram over its own stump. The two-inch difference between the height of undercut and back cut usually prevents this, but you can't depend on it.

As your saw zings through the wood, you wonder when you'll hear that first preliminary warning crack. But before this happens, you might make a thin hardwood wedge to tap into the back cut behind the saw. You saw for a few seconds, drive the wedge deeper, and repeat the sequence. Keep glancing up at the top of the tree to see when it first starts to lean. Probably there'll be some more audible "complaints" along the saw cut as the wood fibers finally begin to tear apart under the enormous stresses that develop in the now-thin strip between the two cuts. Now's the time to holler T-I-M-B-E-R to warn anyone nearby that she's coming down. If you have time, take out your saw; in any case step quickly away along the escape path. As you do, there is a resounding crash and then silence.

There she lies. Why "she"? Our distant ancestors believed that in a tree there lived a nymph, and that what you heard as the tree started to fall was her death cry. In some tribes, a special ritual was performed to placate her spirit. Fig. 17 shows a once-in-a-lifetime discovery. I'm usually death on initial-carvers, but this unknown sculptor certainly captured the mythical idea whether he knew it or not.

You now have the chore of cutting off the branches (limbing). Always start at the butt end and work toward the top. An axe, hatchet, or Sven saw may be used. Cut the branches close to the trunk; only a greenhorn leaves stubs sticking out. If you use an axe, keep checking to see that the path of every swing is clean. Whenever possible, keep the protective trunk between yourself and the branch. In any case, always chop toward the top of the tree.

Some of the branches on the underside of the trunk are often bowed and under great stress. Before you casually swing at one, observe and think what may happen when you clip it from the deceptively inert trunk. I forgot to do this once. The severed branch end whacked me across the chest and knocked me flat on my back. Fortunately, the forest floor was soft, and there were no stubs to impale me as I went down! Instruction in limbing should be one-for-one until the beginner gets quite experienced. There are so many problems that I don't care to keep track of more than one limber at a time.

What to do with the branches? Piled, they make good shelters for rabbits and other critters. Spread out over the ground, they decay faster and become part of the humus layers sooner. But the spread-out method may increase fire danger, and in some forests the piled branches are burned in damp weather when the humus is wet.

The bane of the lumberjack is a "hung-up" tree, one that lodges in another and doesn't fall to the ground. Often, the last strip of wood between the two cuts doesn't break. A couple of clips with the axe may sever it; the tree may then roll one way or the other and finish its fall. If it doesn't, a small tree some four inches in diameter can often be picked up by the butt and snaked away so that the branches untangle and the tree comes the rest of the way down. Keep your feet in the clear! Also, you may be able to throw a rope over the upper part of the trunk and pull it sideways from a safe distance.

Unless you or someone else in camp knows his business, leave large trees for the professional with his power saw. The dangers in felling a tree weighing several tons multiply fast, and this is definitely a hard-hat job. Provided the lean is not excessive, you can usually throw a tree as much as 30° to one side or the other from its natural path by wedging it (a thin magnesium felling wedge can be bought). Also, the rope trick gives good control. You have to get one end of a long ¾-inch-diameter rope fastened to the trunk above its center of gravity. At the other rope end is a three or four-power block-and-tackle attached to another tree or firmly planted post, far enough away so you don't risk pulling the tree down on yourself. Keep a strain on the tackle as you near the end of the back cut. This is a well-controlled procedure. Saw slowly, and keep taking up slack in the rope. You can just about pull even a large tree down where you want it.

Another hazard, especially with larger trees, is the "sailor." When a tree comes crashing down past others, short dead branches are often snapped off and go sailing away. They may have terrific speed and are potentially lethal. Lumberjacks often tell tall tales of mythical forest critters that constantly harass the poor logger. The "agropelter" is a mean, skinny beast with long whiplash arms that lives in treetops. When trees are coming down, he gets so enraged that he grabs a sailor and aims it at the sawyer's head. That's why you should wear a hard hat and keep any observers well away from a falling tree.

Sawing Up

After a tree is felled and limbed, the next step is to "buck" it—cut it into usable lengths or logs. Start at the top, and work toward the butt. Those cross-logs that keep the trunk off the ground now become very important. They may have to be moved because you can't handily saw through an improperly supported section of the trunk. In such spots its weight closes the sawn slot (kerf) and pinches the saw before it goes all the way through. You can drive wedges into the kerf and relieve some

of the pressure, but it's not the best method. If the saw gets pinched, it becomes difficult or impossible to operate; even more important, the pinching may take out the "set" of the cutting teeth. Thereafter, the saw won't run free and easy until the set is restored, which takes special skill and time.

It's much better to place a cross-log so that the length you're sawing off is free and unsupported, or nearly so, at the end. Two people, one on each side, can usually lift the small end of the trunk with long, stout crossed levers so that a cross-log can be placed where needed. If one or more of you decide to just lean over and pick up the trunk end by brute force, remember one thing: never stand up straight and bend at the waist to pick up a weight from the ground. Many millions of human backs have been ruined this way, because their owners didn't know any better. This method puts an enormous stress on the lower vertebrae. When you lift, keep the back as straight as possible, and bend the knees only enough so you can reach the object. Anything too heavy to raise this way is too heavy for you to lift.

Fig. 17: A "wood nymph." Kenneth Fischer "discovered" it and took the photo. He wrote: "I have searched in vain through your dendrology text and can find no variety of beech that fits this phenomenon. And I've looked through H.P. Brown's Textbook of Wood Technology under 'Figure in Wood,' but there's no adequate explanation. Can you enlighten me?"

Two-man Crosscut Sawing

For many years I've introduced this fine team sport of the woodsman to summer campers. It never fails to arouse enthusiasm. On visitor's day at the Sargent College of Physical Education June Camp, we had several dad-daughter teams compete. The senior girls through their Campcraft course were experienced sawyers. The lucky girl was she whose dad happened to have the same sawing rhythm. If you have a group of people all of whom have practiced the same length of time, certain pairs will saw together much better than will the individual partner with someone else. By changing around, a championship pair soon emerges.

Sawing disks from the end of a 12 to 14-inch, medium-soft wood log is a lot of fun, but only when you both know where to stand and how to swing your end of the saw. To stand at the end so that you pull the saw directly toward you is tiring and inefficient. Study Fig. 18 and see that you stand beside the saw and swing it back and forth in front of you. Your whole body sways in rhythm with that of your partner. You can feel instantly any stiffness or lack of coordination on his part. If right-handed, your right hand holds the handle next to the saw with your left hand just above.

In the picture, Mrs. Ken Smith is left-handed, so her left hand is below, right hand above it. Her husband is right-handed and must adapt his position somewhat. Efficiency is best when two "righties" saw together, "lefties" likewise. When sawing coniferous woods (pines, spruces, etc.) or gummy hardwoods such as cherry, lubricate the blade with kerosene.[4]

Crosscut sawing can be pure delight as you pick up the pace, watch the long "chips" pouring from the cut, and catch their aroma as they pile up on the ground. Aldo Leopold called them "fragrant little chips of history...the transect of a century."[5]

Remember that you never push one of these saws. You only pull. Your partner does the same on the return cut. If either of you pushes, the saw buckles and binds in the cut (kerf). In most cases, the weight of the saw itself is enough to saw wood, but experienced sawyers on the return stroke may bear down slightly. This makes the saw "heavier" and faster-cutting, but your partner has to work that much harder to pull it back. Many an old-timer has in this way let his young, green teammate do more than his share!

When starting a cut, one of you may steady the top edge of the saw with his hand in the middle so that the saw starts evenly and doesn't jump out—always a potential danger. After sawing about one-third through, stop and inspect the kerf. Is it perpendicular? Are the edges smooth or ragged? When you first start to saw, have someone stand at one end and glance along the blade's length. Does the saw run straight and true, or does it curve sideways as you pull your stroke? Perhaps you're standing a few inches too far away from the saw and are pulling it toward you instead of straight past. Standing too close may make the saw curve away from you. It must run straight. The disk you saw off tells you how good you are at sawing. The thickness should be about the same throughout, and the surface should be smooth without digs in it. The log you are sawing must rest solidly in a fitted cross-log, or anchored (staked) in some way so that the end is a minimum of six to eight inches off the ground. As you finish the cut, be sure the saw doesn't dip so that its teeth touch the ground.

How you carry one of these saws is of great importance. Never carry it bare with one hand in the center, the teeth pointing up between your arm and body—not even for a few yards. I saw what happened to a student who did this, and I'll never forget it. A bare crosscut saw must be carried flat on one shoulder with the teeth pointing away from you. The arm should be stretched out in front, the hand grasping one of the handles. The other handle can be detached so that it won't snag in the brush along the trail. It is much better to keep the blade "muzzled" when not in use. Cut a one-by-one-inch piece of wood the length of the saw blade. On a table saw, groove this piece from end to end so that it fits easily when placed over the crosscut saw teeth. Tie both ends down. In time, this "scabbard" will conform to the saw's curve (Fig. 19, No. 1).

There are several kinds of crosscut saws. There is the wide-bladed one-man saw with a conventional saw handle on one end, a small attachable two-man handle on the other. For camp use, I don't like it. For about 50 years, I've had a narrow-bladed, lightweight, four-foot, two-man saw, ideal for campers, but you just can't buy one any more. The great saw companies (Atkins, Disston, Simonds) no longer make crosscut saws. The only company that makes the narrow, five-foot-minimum-length saw shown in Fig. 18 is the Jemco Tool Corporation.[6] My preference is the Champion Tooth because of its large size—easier for the beginner to sharpen than the Lance

Tooth, which is smaller and double in number.[7]

When you buy a new saw, you'll find that all the teeth—both the pointed cutters and the notched rakers—are about the same length. The rakers must always be filed shorter than the cutters. If not, the saw will cut very poorly. Fig. 18, No. 2 shows how the rakers work.

To hold the saw, you need a filing board. Get a flat board ¾-inch or more thick, six to eight inches wide, and a couple of inches longer than the saw. Lay the saw (minus handles) on the board so that the center of its toothed curve just reaches the edge away from you. Mark this curve on the board from one end to the other. Remove the crosscut, and,

Fig. 18: 1) Crosscut sawing. 2) Illustration of how a crosscut saw with raker teeth cuts a kerf in timber. (Photo by U.S. Forest Service Equipment Development Center)

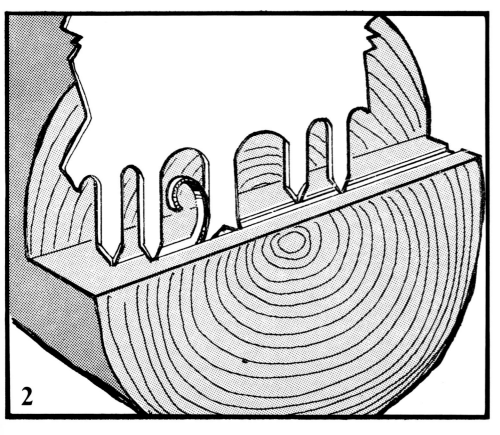

with a hand rip saw or power band saw (this works best), cut to the curve and then smooth it with a plane. Lay the crosscut on the board so that the slots between the teeth extend evenly perhaps ⅛-inch beyond the curved board edge all the way along (Fig. 19, No. 2). Draw a line marking the untoothed edge of the saw, and fasten some narrow cleats as shown. Where the cleats touch the saw, just enough wood is removed from each cleat so that the saw fits snugly between them and the board.

A special saw-filing tool is necessary, whether you have a brand new saw that's never been used or an old one that needs reconditioning. If you can find an old Simonds saw tool somewhere, you're in luck. It does a perfect job. No. 3 shows how to be sure that every tooth (cutters and rakers) is exactly the same height, the entire length of the saw. An eight-inch mill bastard file—teeth pointing forward—has been inserted edgewise under the two lugs, one at each end of the tool. The knurled thumbscrew in the center is tightened until the file has exactly the curve of the teeth from one end of the saw to the other. Hold the tool snugly against the side of the saw, and, using even pressure, push it gently the length of the saw. If the cleats are in the way, first raise the saw and clamp it to the board at each end with C clamps. Of course, the board must be held in a vise at one end, and the other end supported. Inspect each tooth to see whether there's a shiny spot where the file passed over it. The chances are that not all of the teeth were touched. Pick up the tool, turn it around, and, with its face bearing against the other side of the saw, return to the starting point. This "jointing" process is of prime importance. Every tooth must be touched evenly by the file before you proceed further.[8]

When all teeth are the same height, remove the file from the tool. The next step is to file down the rakers. For soft woods, the rakers should be shorter than for hard woods; but a good average difference between cutters and rakers is 1/64 or .016 of an inch.

No. 4 shows the adjustable filing rack at the top, and a raker tooth sticking up ready to be filed to the proper height. Note the scale marks from 0 to 16, each of which is .004 of an inch. To have the rakers 1/64-inch shorter than the cutters, loosen the two thumbscrews and carefully slide the rack until the zero mark (small notch) on the rack is opposite the .016 mark on the scale below (halfway from 0 to 8). The illustration also shows how you can measure

the raker height with a .016-inch thickness (feeler) gauge.

With the thumbscrews tightened, you can now file all the rakers until each is flush with the steel rack. One hand holds the tool firmly against the side of the saw; the other pushes the file. Remove the tool and end clamps, and allow the saw to settle down snugly between the cleats and the board. With a medium-size triangular file, take down the inner two edges of each raker until you barely remove the flat spot—no more or you'll make the raker too short. The file strokes must be at a right angle to the saw face. You can keep checking this by watching a raker as you file it.

The flat mill file is used on the cutters. Notice that in each pair of cutters one has been bent slightly away from you, the other toward you. This is called the "set" and is of great importance. It makes the saw run free and easy. A new saw often retains its precision factory set for some time, unless it's pinched in a log.

File both edges of every cutting tooth that faces *away* from you. Then turn the saw end-for-end, and file the alternate ones that now also face away. Not much filing of the cutters is done in the factory. They don't know whether you'll be sawing soft woods (wide bevel), hard woods (narrow bevel), green wood (wide), or dry wood (narrow). For general camp use, I usually try for a bevel of about 40°, and I file only about the upper third of each tooth—not the full length. Be sure that when you get to a sharp point (or just before it) you stop. If you don't, you'll shorten the tooth![19] When filing these cutters, it's helpful but not necessary to fasten the filing board so that the teeth tilt somewhat away from you. It's very important to have a tight fit between board and saw so that there's no vibration or "chattering" as you file. If there is, use two small C clamps, one on each side, to bring saw and board firmly together. If the files make a horrible screech, you aren't stroking it right. Experiment.

How will you know when the tooth is sharp? Many of us have an overpowering urge to touch it gently to find out. This ain't necessary, and old Cy Lawson, who'd taught thousands of people how to file saws, was death on it. He'd wait until he saw the first finger touch a tooth.

"Boys, stop filing and come here," he'd say. "If you saw a pile of manure there on the ground, you wouldn't go and stick your finger in it to find out what 'twas. You'd use your God-given eyes. Now go

Fig. 19: The crosscut saw. 1) Saw and protective guard. 2) Cleated saw-filing board. 3) Saw-filing tool with flat file (edge view) for making all teeth the same height. 4) Checking height of rakers with thickness gauge.

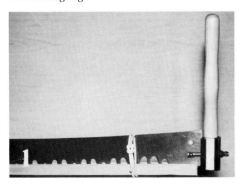
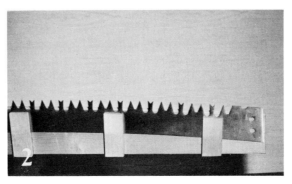

back to work, and keep your fingers off them teeth."

May not be very elegant a warning, but I've remembered it for more than 50 years, and whenever my finger moves toward a newly sharpened tooth, Cy's ghost haunts me!

Finally, as you file tooth after tooth to almost dagger sharpness, I hope you'll develop great respect for that long row of shark's teeth grinning up at you. A sharp tooth on a crosscut saw is no more dangerous than any other sharp tool. But the thing is, there are so many of them. Always keep the guard on the saw when not in use, and to prevent rust, wipe the surfaces with a light oil.

The Peavey

If you have much log rolling to do, you'll need one or two of these excellent tools (Fig. 20). Prior to about 1858, loggers used the primitive "swingdog." At the lower end of a stout staff there was attached, by an eyebolt, a swinging claw which could move not only up and down but also sidewise. This sideways motion made it dangerous to use. One summer's day, according to family records, blacksmith Joe Peavey, having nothing better to do at the moment, was lying on his stomach peering through a crack between two floorboards of a covered bridge. It was nice and cool in there, and he was having fun watching several river men below trying to roll some stranded logs. Suddenly a claw on a swingdog slipped sideways, and the logger was thrown backward into the river. He emerged cursing the so-and-so swingdog.

Joe Peavey saw that a better tool was needed, and like a shaft of light in the darkness of the covered bridge, an idea came to him. He hurried to his smithy and said to his son, "Make me a rigid clasp for a swingdog staff, and bore holes through the lips on the side." Joe then slipped the hole end of a swingdog claw between the two lips and passed a bolt through all three. Now the claw could move up and down but not sidewise. He put some iron collars around the staff below the claw, and drove an iron pick into the end. Next day he gave it to a logger, who soon reported that it was the best log-handling tool ever invented. And so was born the peavey, named after its inventor, and used ever since all over the world.

THE WOODSMAN'S TOOLS

1. Page 34—Henry J. Kauffman has written an excellent history of American axes in *American Axes*. Brattleboro, Vermont: Stephen Greene Press, 1972.

2. Page 40—Such events as speed chopping, it should be said, are purely for recreation. Axemanship has nothing to do with the education of a resource manager or forester. Training for these professions is based solidly on the "mystic" triangle of physics, chemistry, and mathematics. Human relations, ecology, and the other biological and earth sciences are becoming more important as time passes.

3. Page 42—A five-pound Logsplitter Axe is now made that can be used to drive steel wedges and can itself be used as a wedge. The entire head is highly tempered, instead of just the blade. Write the Princeton Company, Box 276, Princeton, MA 01541, for their catalog.

4. Page 46—People like to save the disks cut from a log as souvenirs. But as the disks dry, they usually crack. To help prevent this, soak them for several weeks in a polyethylene-glycol-water solution. Four pounds of the chemical in five quarts of water makes seven quarts. For details of this treatment, write the U.S. Forest Products Laboratory, Madison, WI.

5. Page 46—Aldo Leopold, *A Sand Country Almanac, and Sketches Here and There,* New York: Oxford University Press, 1974.

6. Page 46—For the narrow crosscut saw, write the Jemco Tool Corporation, Seneca Falls, NY 13148.

7. Page 47—For a general discussion of crosscut saws, write the U.S. Forest Service, Equipment Development Center, Missoula, MT 59801, and ask for a copy of their booklet, "Crosscut Saw Manual."

8. Page 48—The Century Tool Company, Ginkgo Industrial Park, Ivyland, PA 18974, makes a modern version of the Simonds tool. The one I purchased had no zero mark on the rack; hence the thickness-feeler gauge shown in the illustration.

9. Page 48—How to set a saw is described in Warren Miller, "Crosscut Saw Manual."

Fig. 20: Modern version of Joe Peavey's famous invention that made log handling much safer.

A PIECE OF WOOD

For anyone who has never seen a thin section of wood through a microscope, its marvelously beautiful structure can scarcely be imagined. Even with a pocket magnifying lens, one can enter a whole new world by observing an end section of a piece of wood that has been smoothly cut with a sharp knife or a razor blade.

The picture on the left in Fig. 21 is of white pine wood. You can see six complete growth rings, and parts of two more at the top and bottom of the photo. Usually a growth ring is formed each year. The "holes" are resin canals found in many conifers. Resin canals are especially large in the pines; if you sit on a fresh pine stump you'll learn first-hand just how sticky the resin can be. In the center of the photo a vertical dark line runs from top to bottom.

This is a wood ray, in which food is stored. See how much wider the rays are in the maple and oak.

The beautiful lace-like structure of pine wood is made up of millions of tiny cells. These cells are fibers, many times longer than they are wide. To see them, just tear a piece of paper and look at the torn edge. Wood fibers separated chemically or by grinding are the raw material for the giant paper, pulp, and cellulose industries. The fiber cross sections in maple and oak are so much narrower that they are barely if at all visible in the photos.

Notice that the maple and oak have small or large holes of a kind not found in the pine. Sap in the pine goes up through the closed fibers, which have little connecting valves along their overlapping ends. In maple and oak, the holes are the cut ends of long tubes, the "plumbing" that carries most of the sap. All three pictures are placed so that their bottom edges are toward the center of the tree—direction of growth is from the bottom to the top of the photos. Notice that in the pine, the fibers at the beginning of each year's growth or earlywood are relatively large—sap is running fast. As autumn approaches, the latewood fibers are much smaller radially. In maple, the sap tubes are scattered throughout the ring. The wood is thus diffuse porous. In oak, which is ring porous, enormous tubes are found in the earlywood, and only a few small ones appear in the latewood, which is mostly made up of very small thick-walled fibers which give great strength to the wood. The earlywood pores in oak are so large that you can see them as "grain" in an oak floor. In red oak the pores are so empty that you can take a one-by-one-inch piece of the wood a foot long, dip one end in soap suds or detergent, blow on the other end and produce a mass of soap bubbles! (Fig. 22 shows the very latest way to view the beautiful structure of a piece of wood.)[1]

An important thing about ring-porous woods such as oak, ash, and hickory, is the relative strength of the earlywood and latewood. That row of large tubes is weak compared to the dense heavy fibers of the latewood. It so happens that in ring-porous woods, no matter how fast or slow their growth, the number of earlywood pores is about the same. The variable part of the ring is the heavy strong latewood. So if you want a strong piece of hickory, look at the rings on the end, and see that they are perhaps one-eighth of an inch wide or even wider.

As you look at the three pictures it should be clear that the less air space there is in wood structure, the heavier and therefore the stronger the wood will be. Compared with the weight of water (1.00), the relative weight of white pine is about .35, of sugar maple .60, and of red oak also .60. This assumes that they are all of the same dryness, in this case with a moisture content of 15 percent.

Before going any further, we must know what is meant by "softwoods" and "hardwoods." The wood of any conifer (mostly needle-leaved evergreens) is called a *softwood,* and that of the broadleaved trees is a *hardwood.* Nearly all of the conifers are evergreen, while most of the broadleaved trees lose their leaves in autumn. Softwoods have no pores; hardwoods do have them (look at the pictures again). Most softwoods actually have soft wood (some pines, spruces, firs, etc.), and most hardwoods have hard wood (maples, oaks, hickories, etc.); but there are many exceptions. For instance,

the southern softwood longleaf pine has hard wood, while any number of hardwoods (basswood, poplar, tuliptree, buckeye, and others) have soft wood!

One of the most practical things to know about various woods is how they behave in a campfire.[2] Any wood should be as dry as possible. Water must be driven off before a piece of green or wet wood burns, and this wastes heat energy from your fire. The following table lists a number of woods to show their relative fuel value. Since the weight of wood in a species varies from tree to tree, and even in different parts of the same tree, the average weights listed cannot be exact. Also, several of the names listed (hickory, oak, ash, and others) include several to many separate species. These data are courtesy of U.S. Forest Products Laboratory, Madison, Wisconsin.

Fig. 21: Cross sections of wood enlarged about 20 times. From left: white pine, sugar maple, red oak.

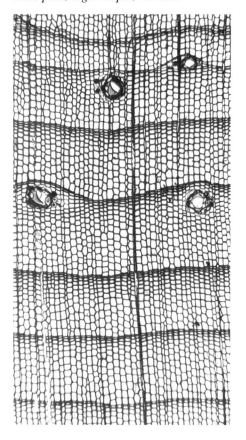 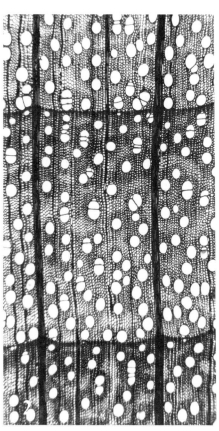 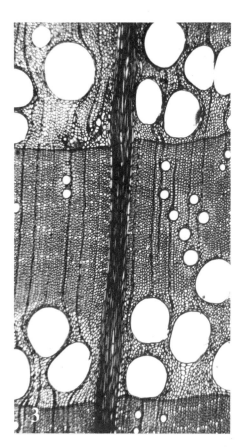

Relative Fuel Value of Some Common Woods
at 15% Moisture Content, Hickory taken as 100%

Kind of Wood	Average Weight per Cubic Foot	Heat Value in per-cent
Hickory	50.3 lbs.	100
Flowering dogwood	50.3	100
Black locust	52.0	103
Hophornbeam	49.4	98
Apple	47.7	95
American hornbeam (Blue-beech)	45.2	90
Oak (red)	43.5	86
Maple (sugar)	43.5	86
Beech	43.5	86
Birch	42.6	85
Ash (except black)	41.0	81
Walnut (black)	39.3	78
Southern hard pine	38.5	76
Elm	38.5	76
Maple (red)	37.6	75
Tamarack	37.6	75
Black cherry	36.0	72
Black tupelo (blackgum)	35.2	70
Sycamore	35.2	70
Sweetgum (redgum)	35.2	70
Douglas-fir	34.4	68
Sassafras	32.0	64
Baldcypress	32.0	64
Hemlock (western)	32.0	64
Yellow-poplar (tuliptree)	30.3	60
Catalpa	28.7	57
Spruce	27.9	56
Cottonwood	27.9	56
Red alder	27.9	56
Redwood	27.2	54
Willow	27.2	54
Aspen	27.2	54
Balsam fir	25.6	51
White pine	25.6	51
Basswood	24.0	48
White-cedar	22.4	45

It's easy to see that the heavier a piece of dry wood is, the more fuel value it has. This is because there is actually more wood substance there. Look at the three pictures again. White pine fibers are relatively thin-walled. Most of the wood is air space. In both hard maple and oak, the fact that their hollow tubes are air spaces is more than offset by the dense, thick-walled fibers of the remaining wood structure. Other important information about firewood is found on p. 62.

The table is useful also to find out the relative strength of a wood at a standard moisture content. This parallels the fuel value, because again, in general, the more actual wood substance there is, the greater the strength. Both oak and hickory are very strong, black cherry and sycamore are somewhere in the middle, and the wood of aspen and California redwood is relatively weak.

The resistance of wood to decay bears no relation to its actual weight. First of all, the sapwood of most logs soon decays if the logs are left in the woods or stored in a moist place. It is the heartwood that may resist wood-destroying fungi. This is because some kinds of trees have in the heartwood accumulated tannins, oils, or other chemicals that are poisonous to fungi. The heartwood of California redwood, although relatively light in weight and weak, has almost unbelievable durability because of its tannins. Tree trunks lying on the ground for a thousand years or more are often still sound. Hickory heartwood, heavy and very strong, decays within a few years. The following table should be useful in planning, building, and maintaining your camp structures. Remember that any *dry* wood practically lasts forever. Your permanent buildings must be built so that they shed water. There must not be places where water can collect and seep into the wood. This invites decay. Wood should not be nearer to the ground than eight inches, and good cross ventilation between earth and the ground floor must be provided.[3]

These woods on the right are listed alphabetically, and are definitely not in order of decay resistance in each group. Also, because of the great variability of wood itself and the conditions under which it might be used—to say nothing of the selectivity of certain fungi in attacking some woods but not others—these listings must be considered only as estimates. However, if this is understood, the table is still useful, especially in comparing woods with high resistance with those of low or almost no resistance.

Relative Resistance of Heartwood to Decay
(Adapted from U.S. Forest Products Lab.,
Tech. Note 229, 1961)

High	Intermediate	Low
Baldcypress (old growth)	Baldcypress (young growth)	Alder, red
Catalpa	Douglas-fir	Ashes
Cedars	Honeylocust	Aspens
Chestnut	Larch, western	Basswood
Cypress, Arizona	Pine, eastern white	Beech
Junipers	Pines, southern	Birches
Locust, black	Tamarack	Buckeye
Mulberry, red		Butternut
Oaks, white (most)		Cottonwoods and other poplars
Osage-orange		Elms and hackberry
Redwood		Hemlocks
Sassafras		Hickories
Walnut, black		Maples
Yew, Pacific		Oaks, red
		Pines (most others)
		Spruces
		Sweetgum
		Sycamore
		Willows
		Yellow-poplar

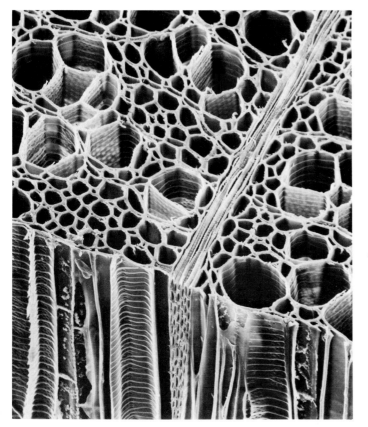

Fig. 22: Wood structure of basswood enlarged 300 times by an electron scanning microscope. Never before have we been able actually to look down into a block of wood and see its beautiful structure in three dimensions. The vertical diagonal cut from left to right allows us to see both the cross section (upper two thirds) and the tangential section (lower third) at the same time. (Photo by N.C. Brown Center for Ultrastructure Studies, SUNY College of Environmental Science and Forestry.)

A PIECE OF WOOD

1. Page 52—For more about wood, see William M. Harlow, *Inside Wood, Masterpiece of Nature.* Washington, DC: The American Forestry Association, 1970.

2. Page 53—The U.S. Forest Service at Upper Darby, PA 19082, will send you a folder, "Enjoy Your Fireplace, Especially During the Energy Crisis." Although it has to do with indoor fireplaces, much of the information is also applicable to building outdoor woods fires.

3. Page 54—For detailed information on using wood in outdoor structures, write the U.S. Forest Products Laboratory, P.O. Box 5130, North Walnut St., Madison, WI 53705.

FIRE

Around the cave entrance stand great tree trunks, part of the dense broadleaf forest that by day shuts out the sunlight so that a hunter looking for food travels in perpetual twilight. At night there is only inky blackness, except for an occasional star peering through the leafy canopy overhead. In front of the cave, the magic fire burns brightly, casting enormous, mysterious shadows. A man crouches behind it and carefully adds a few sticks. The fire is so hungry. Years before, the man learned what a large pile of wood it would eat in just one night. From behind him, he listens to the sleep sounds of his family, lulled by the reflected warmth from the fire.

This man was our ancestor of perhaps 50,000 years ago. Is there a universal and continuing consciousness about fire and other primitive things,

running like a thread from those ancient days to each one of us today? Fire still makes its magic in countless millions of fireplaces, both outside and inside. The fireplace may no longer be essential for heat and light, but its fire forever renews the spirit of those who gaze into it. Fire under control is a great servant and friend—but allowed to escape, it is a terrifying enemy that man can never forget.

It is hard to imagine a camping trip without the delicious aroma and taste of food properly cooked over an open fire. And it is unthinkable not to have an evening campfire lighting up one small circle in the darkness of the surrounding forest. However, the great pressure of too many people on a limited number of campsites has in some places made it almost impossible to enjoy the priceless benefits of a campfire. Portable camp stoves, light enough to pack, are increasing in number. Fortunately, there are still vast areas of American wilderness where one may build his fire. And in organized summer camps, there is every reason to keep up the campfire tradition.

Camp Fires

On trips away from an established campsite with its fireplaces, you must always know whether permission is necessary to build a fire. Even at regular campsites, a fire permit may be required; on private land, permission must always be obtained in advance of your trip.

In the forest, the ground is covered by three layers of fallen leaves, twigs, bits of bark, and down trees, all in various stages of decay. At the surface is *litter,* or recognizable dead matter. Below the litter is *duff,* compacted, partly decayed organic material. Under the duff is *humus,* black, almost completely decayed organic matter. These layers feel springy underfoot.

A fire must never be built upon this covering of dead matter, not even on the nearly black underlayer, which many people do not bother to remove before starting a fire. You must remove all of this organic matter right down to the mineral soil (sand, clay, rock). Fire in the black stuff may smolder for days and then break out into a full-fledged forest fire. I have seen fire pits dug down to mineral soil with the humus layer left all around the edge of the pit. The digger had put an inch or two of mineral soil on top of the humus, and then placed rocks on top of the whole. This is about the worst thing you can do. Even though the fire in the pit is put out, there may be still-glowing patches in the humus, ready to spread perhaps days after you are gone. To be reasonably safe, the humus must be completely removed from a circle about 10 feet in diameter. Under continually moist conditions, this may be more than needed; but where the woods are tinder-dry after months of drought, even a small fire in the center of a 10-foot circle may be risky, especially if there is a strong wind.

In broadleaf deciduous forests of the eastern United States and elsewhere, the fallen leaves decompose rather quickly, and one finds mineral soil under a shallow, easily removed layer of humus. But in dense coniferous woods, the duff layer can be very deep; if so, it makes no sense to try to clear it away so that a fire can be built with safety. Try for the sandy margin of a river or lake, or a rocky area with no vegetation.

Just what is fire? For many years I've astonished people by saying, "Wood itself doesn't burn." It has to be heated until flammable gases are given off and mixed with oxygen. A wood fire is an enormously complex series of chemical reactions in which the flaming gases give off heat and light and yield carbon dioxide and water. These are the very substances that the green leaves have used, with the sun's captured energy, to form the sugars that built the tree's woody body so long ago. If you burn wood from the center of a 250-year-old oak tree, you liberate to the atmosphere carbon and water that the tree took from it before the American Revolution. Near the center of an ancient Sequoia, these materials may have been locked up since before the birth of Christ—and in the oldest bristlecone pines, for 4,000 to nearly 5,000 years.

Besides fuel in gaseous form, there must be oxygen and something hot enough to start the fire reaction. Remove any one of these three elements,

Fig. 23: Two kinds of match safes.

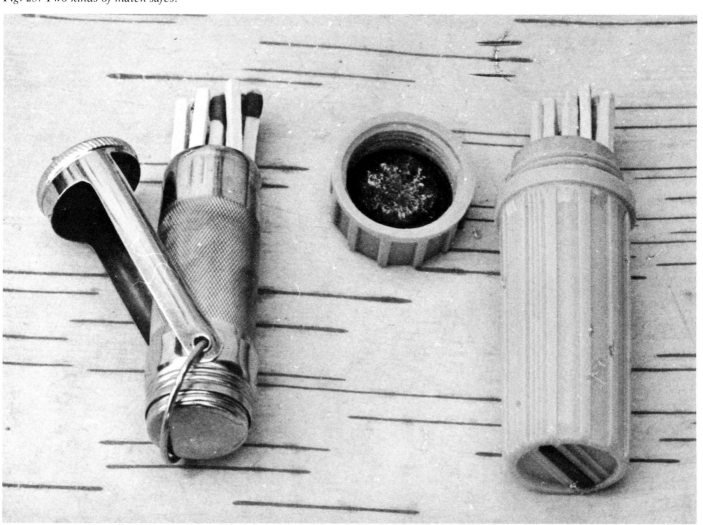

and there will be no fire. This is important to remember. Where do you suppose "Don't be a wet blanket" came from? A wet blanket puts out fire by smothering it. Not only is oxygen cut off but also the temperature is lowered below the flash point (minimum burning temperature) of the gases. The gas flames furnish from one-half to two-thirds of the heat given off by a wood fire. The rest of the heat comes from the glowing coals.

Now to the practical: how do you actually build a fire in the woods? When everything is bone-dry, not much skill is needed; anyone can do it. After a long rainstorm or in the rain, it's a different matter entirely.

Matches. The match is the usual flame maker. The paper matches in books are not worth considering; they're too short and fragile, and they burn too quickly. The longer wooden ones in small boxes are better, especially if they are the waterproof kind. The old standby is the wooden kitchen match, 2½ inches long. To improve its flame for woods use, tie bundles of about a dozen each, and push them under in melted paraffin until they cease bubbling. (Use the greatest care in handling hot paraffin. It should be heated to just above its melting point, no hotter. Use only enough to cover the bundles of matches. Improper use of paraffin leads to danger of fire.) Dry the matches at once on a paper towel.

You want impregnation but no excess paraffin, especially on the head. An excess may make the match more difficult to light. When they're cool, strike some of your treated matches and compare the flame with that from untreated ones. Whether treated or not, matches must be kept in an absolutely watertight container. The simplest is a small plastic bag gathered and folded at the top, tightly pinched with a rubber band. Matches so contained should be weighted down under water. Watch carefully for a string of bubbles. They mean that your arrangement is no good. Otherwise, leave submerged overnight. Dry, and open the bag. Any dampness? Will the matches light? Personally, I don't care to trust my life to any little old plastic bag. There are vast areas in the arid West, however, where such protection is enough—unless you're traveling on the water with the chance of an upset.

Not too many types of waterproof match safes are advertised. Fig. 23 shows two good ones. The metal "Marbles" safe has a rubber disk in the top; when the barrel is swung in and turned, it makes a perfect seal. Unless one knows its opening "secret," it is also quite tamper-proof. The crisscross pattern on the outside is supposed to provide a good striking surface, but several quick, firm passes may be needed to ignite the match. It's much better to cut a strip of medium-grit, waterproof emery paper that fits (grit side out) inside your match box. Use it only when nothing else is handy. Old-timers may strike matches on the seat of their pants—but not when everything, including themselves, is soaking wet. The orange plastic match safe has a rubber sealing disk in the cap, and a circular striker of emery paper. It floats in water; the metal one sinks. Both safes hold about 15 kitchen matches.

You must carry such an emergency supply on your person at all times when in the wild. It may be a matter of life or death. For day-to-day use, you can carry a few bundles of the paraffin-treated matches in a plastic bag. Years ago, we used to fill a box of kitchen matches with melted paraffin. From the hardened block we could break out matches as needed. You'll still find this method in the books. Don't trust it until you've checked it out. I've tried it with today's matches. I couldn't light a single one! Several campers have told me that the kitchen match "ain't what it used to be." However, I still think it's the best bet.

There is on the market an item called a Metal Match. By bearing down on it with a piece of steel (furnished), you can strike a spark just as you might with flint and steel, the old pioneer way. If you get one of these, be sure to experiment with it and learn its quirks before adding it to your emergency kit.

Tinder. This originally meant something that would ignite and smolder when struck by a spark from flint and steel. Here, tinder is anything that catches fire readily from the flame of a match. Over the vast areas where birches and their papery bark are common, birch bark is supreme for starting a fire. The old woodsman may carry a little roll of it in his pocket or cook kit just in case there is none around at the next campsite. The paper birch of the northland often makes available naturally shed pieces of the outer bark. Back in the woods away from trails or campsites, you can pick off a handful of yellow birch curls without making the tree unsightly. But never cut into a live birch tree for its bark. Underneath the outer papery layers is a green layer of living inner bark. In time, when exposed, this turns into a black, unsightly ring around the tree.

Fig. 24: Tinder. 1) Bark of yellow birch burns fiercely. 2) Compacted dead twigs of conifers are quick to ignite. 3) Burning "frill" sticks of a softwood are good starters. 4) A piece of southern "lightwood" (resinous pine) is also an excellent fire starter.

Fig. 24, No. 1 shows just how flammable birch bark is. In this case it was yellow birch, two pieces picked up from the damp forest floor. They had once encased the wood of a fallen branch that had long since rotted away. I have even set a rotted six-inch-long yellow-birch segment on end and lighted the bark at the bottom. The bark flared up and burned away, leaving the wet rotted core inside! Sometimes, if everything is too wet, this doesn't work, but in general birch bark burns like tarpaper. The bark contains natural flammable oils and resins.

No. 2 shows some closely spaced, dead twigs of a conifer. After lighting them in two places, I blew out the kitchen match and left it in the picture to show how big the twigs were; many beginners waste time chewing up tinder into little pieces a couple of inches long. They don't stack as well as longer ones. Small, dead twigs on the lower trunk of a live tree are relatively dry. They are sheltered from moderate rain by the leaf cover overhead. After the rain, they dry quickly in the breezes that sweep through the forest. If you just collect a handful and crisscross them on the ground, there will be too much air space between them. The pile may not catch fire. You must squeeze them together into fagots, which are then broken into about eight-inch lengths and piled closely together as shown. Air space is important, but more than one-eighth of an inch between fagots is too much.

There are many other things that can be used for tinder: dry weed tops in autumn, grapevine bark, and—for those who don't appreciate the true woodland experience—toilet paper. When everything is bone-dry, dead leaves may do, but most of them are damp, good only for a smudge to discourage biting insects.

No. 3 illustrates the old standby "frill" sticks (see also p. 27), whittled preferably from a soft wood. A few of these sticks stacked close together will catch fire at once when touched by a flaming match. All through the great pine forests of the southeastern U.S., resin-soaked pine stumps of trees that have been turpentined (worked for naval stores) yield "lightwood" (No. 4). When split pieces, even an inch across, are touched with a flame, they start to burn fiercely, and soon the whole piece is a flaming torch. In other regions where there are pines, you can often tear out old resinous branch ends or knots from a decayed trunk. These are good fire starters as well as emergency torches.

In this chemical age you can buy man-made starters, such as flammable tablets and a ribbon that is squeezed out of a tube like toothpaste. I don't think a woodsman needs to buy such things. Somehow it spoils the challenge.

To Build a Fire

A lot of foolishness has been written about this soul-satisfying and practical art. One would think that certain "fire lays" are essential for success. Above the tinder you must build a "tipi" or a "log cabin" before lighting the match. Look at Fig. 25, No. 1. Because fire runs up a slanting stick faster than along a horizontal one, it makes sense to have piled the tinder in a rough cone and to lay the sticks on in a similar way all around. You may be instructed by some manuals to complete such a lay before lighting the tinder. But more than once, I've lighted the tinder and been dismayed to have it flare up and go out, leaving the smoldering kindling with little flame and much smoke. "Not enough tinder," you say, "Kindling sticks too big, everything damp."

Probably, but many an old woodsman who never read a book does it differently. He sets up his tinder and places a few small sticks against it. He has beside him plenty of small stuff to add instantly when he sees just how the fire develops. Often, an already completed pile doesn't catch fire uniformly; part of it may even burn out, leaving the rest of it smoldering. Of course, if wind is a factor, kindling is placed on the leeward side. In less time than it took to write about this method, the old woodsman has a dandy little blaze going, and can quickly make it grow to the size needed. Tending a fire is an art learned by long experience.

To go back a bit—before striking the match, take a few seconds to study the arrangement of the tinder. This is most important, especially with stacked fine twigs or whittled frill sticks. You can't just stick the burning match into the base of the pile anywhere and be successful. Often, there will be only one or two places to windward where the feeble flame of the match will best ignite the little twigs or shavings so that the fire spreads quickly throughout the pile. Think and observe as the miracle begins. Remember that twigs too close together burn poorly. But if they're too far apart, the lighted ones flame up and go out; the tiny flames do not reach across the spaces and ignite the other twigs next to them.

Having decided where to light the tinder, you now crouch or kneel and strike the match. It's amusing to read in the books about which way to face. Some say toward the wind, others away from it! I kneel with my back to the wind, strike the match, and as it flares, quickly shift it between thumb and forefinger so that it slants down and the flame is sheltered by both of my cupped hands. As it begins to run up the match stick, I light the tinder at the place chosen, and if possible also at another one before the match burns down to my fingers. This is why the longer, larger-diameter kitchen matches are better than the shorter ones sold in small boxes.

No matter how you place the sticks on your new fire, they'll soon burn down to coals and ashes (No. 2) unless you keep adding fuel. At this point or before, you may prefer to change over to a "criss-cross" arrangement, No. 3. The slant-stick fire lay concentrates the heat in one spot under a kettle for the northern woodsman's noonday boil for his cup of tea or for a one-pot meal. The crisscross is better when you want a larger area of heat.

No. 4 shows the Indian's "star fire," an excellent arrangement. You can use sticks of any length up to four feet or more. Just keep pushing the ends in as they burn away. This saves a lot of chopping or sawing. Remember, saving your energy is most important when you're traveling or camping in the woods. The disadvantage of the star fire is that in working around it you must be extra careful

Fig. 25: Building a fire. 1) Wood added to the fire shown in Fig. 24, No. 3. 2) The fire has burned out and collapsed, leaving coals. 3) Criss-cross fire built on these coals. 4) Indian star fire.

not to upset things by kicking one of the sticks or stepping on a "roller" that may give you a fall.

Important Firecraft Pointers

1. Gather enough wood so that you don't have to leave the fire untended even for one minute. If there are two or more campers, someone must watch the fire at all times. The others can go for more wood.

2. If at all possible, keep a full bucket of water standing by before you strike the match.

3. In choosing a fire site in the woods, be sure there are no overhanging branches that might be scorched or burned.

4. *Never* build a fire against a tree trunk or a log lying on the ground! (It's been done.)

5. A "persuader" (a foot-long rubber or aluminum tube, or an elder sprout with the pith punched out) is handy to blow a stream of air at the base of a lazy fire to get it going.

6. Always keep the fire small. If you can't squat within two or three feet of it, it's probably too big. Big fires waste fuel and are more dangerous.

7. Split wood catches fire more quickly than does round wood of the same size. Splitting produces edges and slivers that heat through and give off flammable gases sooner than a round piece.

8. As wood burns, a layer of charcoal forms on the outside. The charcoal is an excellent heat insulator, and it reduces the speed of burning. This is one reason for poking a fire—it knocks off the charcoal layer and opens up unburned wood inside.

Firewood

Selecting firewood is an art. The branches of an old fallen dead tree may be good. Of course, they must be sticking up or out from the trunk, and not lying on wet ground. Bare branches are apt to be drier and less decayed than those with the bark still on. Try kicking one to see whether it's still sound, or breaks off, half-decayed or punky. Soggy, decayed wood is no good except to make a smudge. Kephart's classic *Camping and Woodcraft* lists a number of woods, indicating their relative fire value and burning characteristics.[1] A few of them burn almost as well green, right out of the tree, as when dry. White ash is outstanding.

On a wager, Kephart cut a small white ash, sectioned and split it to small size, whittled a few frill sticks, and with one match soon had a hot little fire going. Scarcely believing this, I tried it—with the same happy result! Unless it means unacceptable danger, never believe what you read in books until you try it yourself. The burning characteristics of a wood grown in the southern Appalachians, for instance, may or may not be the same as those of identical species in Minnesota or Maine. Then too, rapidity of growth, time of year, moisture content in particular, and other things in general all have an effect.

Fire in the Wet

All of the above assumes that things are dry or just a little moist. What will you do when everything is soaking wet? Can you build a fire in the rain? This is the ultimate challenge, unless of course it's winter at 40° below zero. First of all, you need some sort of temporary shelter overhead. This can be a 5 × 5-foot piece of plastic sheet supported at the corners by four poles, two at one side slightly shorter than the other two for drainage, the whole thing guyed with binder twine.

Following Kephart and many another woodsman, try to find a dead, sound, leaning (preferably softwood) trunk. Chop into the underside at a slant, springing off small slabs that you hope are dryish. You can split the slabs finer under your canopy. In birch country, birch bark with any surface water mopped off will catch fire and ignite the split kindling you've piled over it. So too will "lightwood" or pine knots. You will already have collected a good supply of dead branches and slanted them up on a live tree trunk so that they will drain off what rain comes through the green leaves overhead.

I prefer a lean-to lay with a back-log or stones behind to support the upper ends of the sticks. Once your fire is started, get as many of the other sticks on as possible (observing air space) without smothering the fire underneath. A fire will burn quite well in the rain if you can keep it covered with a roof of wood pieces that shed most of the water but leave all-important air spaces. The longer the fire burns and the more hot coals form underneath, the better it works. The covered wet lengths dry out and burn while you add more wet sticks on top. Be careful not to burn your plastic roof, which may be removed when the fire gets going.

One time my wife and I were marooned for three days on a small, uninhabited island in the upper St. Lawrence River. The nor'west gale had a 20-mile fetch, and waves four to five feet high crashed

Fig. 26: The fireplace. 1) Double arrangement allows kettles to be placed anywhere desired. 2) Two green sticks support fry pan over coals. 3) Grill from an old refrigerator. Never cook food directly on one of these racks. The older ones may be cadmium-plated, and therefore poisonous.

against the rocky shore. It rained most of the time. Even though we were travelling in one of the best sea boats ever built—the Thousand Island skiff—we decided to wait for the gale to blow itself out. We had a snug camp—a homemade open baker tent facing the fire. There was plenty of dead standing white ash about, and we kept that fire going day and night. The rock wall fireback reflected welcome heat into the tent. It quit raining the fourth day. The rollers were still pretty large, but we shoved off anyway. We reduced sail and had an exciting 10-mile voyage downwind back to civilization.

Putting It Out

When everything is soaking wet, you can leave a fire going all night, to reflect heat from backlogs into your shelter. But in many cases in arid country or during a drought anywhere, this may be suicidal. Assuming the fire has burned down to coals and ashes, tip the bucket and splash water with your hand all over the surface and around the edges until it stops hissing. Then take a stick and stir the coals. Turn over any partly burned sticks and soak them. If you've used someone else's fireplace, push back the rocks and soak the edges all around. Before starting the fire, you should have checked to be sure no humus was hiding somewhere around these edges. Lay the flat of your hand on the wet ashes until you've tested the whole area.

Suppose you have no water. The somewhat cooled, spread-out coals and ashes can be well covered with mineral soil (dirt, sand, or clay). But never forget that fire buried this way is still alive for hours, or even a day or two afterward. Far better, plan to stay there an hour or more, until you can thrust your hand into cold ashes; then cover them. The last responsibility of the leader is to see that the fire is really out before the group leaves the camp-site.

Fire and Cooking

This is a vast subject, with scores of books giving hundreds of recipes. My main interest is how to manage and contain your fire, Fig. 26. If you want to hang several kettles over the fire in traditional fashion, you drive a couple of forked stakes at either end, place a green "lug" stick across them, and hang the kettles from pothooks. Use fairly hard wood that will bear the cut of a deep, slanting notch near the base. Try fitting the bail of your kettle into this notch. The cut must be deep enough so that the

kettle bail can never slip out when you move the pothook and kettle, with its boiling contents, along the lug stick. There are several other ways to make pothooks. Notice the kettle at the left end hanging from a straightened coat hanger in the photo. The heavy wire of these hangers has all sorts of uses in camp.

I'm always amused to see artists' drawings of the forked stakes. They are usually shown with a "Y" top. How do you drive such a thing? Besides, it's uncommon even to find a "Y". Most of our trees have alternate branching and don't form "Y"s. However, in any case, if the ground is too hard, it's easier to sharpen a short stake to start the holes. Then the forked stakes can be driven or pushed in firmly. Notice that the rear pair are straight, and have side branches that hold the lug stick. It's not even necessary to have a fork at all. Notice that the left front stake is split, and the flattened lug stick is wedged into it; at the other end, just a firm lashing of binder twine holds the two sticks together.

By now you'll have noticed the "double rig," with two lug poles instead of one. The Chippewa used this method to hang pails of maple sap over the fire in making sugar. I find the rig very handy. With it you can get any degree of heat you wish—the kettles can be moved both lengthwise and cross-wise. When cooking is finished, the lug stick ("waugan" stick of the Indians) must be removed. According to backwoods lore, it's bad luck to leave it in place.[2]

The three pictures in Fig. 26 illustrate the old saying "flames for boiling, hot coals for frying." When building a fireplace, you should keep the tops on each side as level as possible; the grill, if you use one, should also be leveled. It's most annoying to see the food on one side of your pan dry and burning while the other half of your meal is swimming in excess cooking oil. The height of your fireplace sides is important. I've seen fireplaces in public picnic grounds 12 inches or more from grill to earth. This requires more fuel than necessary. Eight or nine inches in height should be enough. When rocks are scarce, you can use fewer and dig out some of the dirt between the two fireplace sides. Of course, the fireplace should be built to take advantage of the prevailing wind, if there is one, so that you get a good draft.

The kind of rocks you use for a fireplace may be important. Layered ones, especially sandstone (a sedimentary rock, laid down at the bottom of some ancient sea) are suspect because they may hold enough moisture to explode when heated. However, I've built fireplaces of layered limestone over a period of some 60 years and have never had an explosion—only an occasional harmless "pop" or two. If you're concerned about this, or can't find rocks of any sort, you can make a "Nessmuk" Kitchen—provided you are allowed to cut a green sappy hardwood tree at least four inches in diameter, Fig. 27. The round tops should be hewed flat to support cooking utensils safely. The inner faces also should be flattened to give more room for the fire. Some of the dirt between the logs is dug out and used to level and embed them. Looking at Fig. 27, you can see that the logs, after being used a few times, get eaten away by fire. They can then be moved closer together. The pan may look to be precariously supported, but it actually is still quite stable.[3]

For a one-pot meal, nothing as complicated as either of these arrangements is needed. Perhaps a couple of rocks with flat tops and the fire between them, or a trench in the earth, will do. The hobo's single dingle stick with the base stuck in the ground and the slant adjusted with a rock underneath has never appealed to me. It seems too unstable. If you can find one stick, you can probably find three for a tripod lashed with binder twine. A length of aluminum chain or a straightened coat hanger can suspend the pot.

With any arrangement, have the pot or other utensils for boiling in place over your fire lay before striking the match. In this way you use all the heat possible, even that from the blazing tinder.

Buffalo Steak Roast

I was introduced to this method of broiling steak nearly 30 years ago by Cap'n Bill Vinal. He learned it from the incomparable naturalist, woodsman, and master storyteller, Ernest Thompson Seton. Presumably, Seton got it from the Indians.

This method is the proper one for cooking steak over coals. I have never used any other since I first saw it done. This very strong statement will be challenged by the more than 50 million backyard chefs who may never have seen a properly cooked steak, and who imagine that we should enjoy eating meat that is coated with tar residues from the action of blazing fat dripping on half-burned charcoal.

Fig. 27: 1) A Nessmuk kitchen. 2) Tripod fastened with binder twine. Base ends must be firmly set into ground.

Steak should not be supported on a grill *over* the coals. It should be pushed down directly *on* them after they have turned white with ash. Immediately push some coals up around the edges of the steak to keep out as much air as possible. To those who have never cooked a steak this way, the whole idea is horrifying. Surely your beautiful, expensive steak will be burned to a crisp!

Actually, nothing of the kind happens. When you remove the steak, after five to seven minutes, its underside will be gray and not blackened anywhere, except perhaps at one or two places around the edge where the coals did not touch. Before cooking the other side, stir up the coals a bit so that those that have done their work and look black are replaced with fresh, hot, glowing coals from underneath. After putting the steak back on, you can knock off the few coals that stick to the now-cooked top side. The times I've given are for a one-inch-thick steak, which will be gray throughout, or pink in the center. Change the time to suit your taste.

Meanwhile, melt some butter or margarine in a baking pan. When the second side of the steak is done, lift it off, knock off any sticking coals, and place it in the baking pan. Carve it into strips about 1½ inches wide, and let it simmer for a few minutes. If you find the inside too pink, turn the strips up on edge to finish cooking. Meantime, you can have opened and toasted some ordinary hamburger rolls. Dip the flat sides into the delicious gravy, insert a strip of the meat, and hand it to one of the hungry "wolves" hovering around you!

One important thing should be mentioned. To cook steak this way, all excess fat, especially around the edges, must be cut away. The heat from the fire will set fat ablaze almost at once. On a sirloin, fat removal may leave a tail piece that's difficult to handle. A couple of skewers can be used to pin this piece to the main body to make a compact whole.

Cap'n Bill, L.B. Sharp, and I have cooked steaks for 30 or more people using this method. The campers are organized into five groups: wood gatherers, fire tenders, steak trimmers and tossers, steak turners and charcoal knockers, and carvers. The "Roast Master" will know from experience how much good, dry, sound, hard hardwood is needed, and will see that the wood gatherers bring in enough —much more than you might think necessary to make a bed of coals three inches deep. A shallow trench long enough for the number of steaks to be broiled is scooped out. If you prefer, the trench may be circular.

Depending on the size of the firewood, the fire is lighted from one to 1½ hours before steak time. Sticks more than three inches in diameter take too long to burn down. I have been surprised to find that even pieces one-half to one inch thick produce a good bed of coals. If the trench is long, several fires may be lighted along it, with the larger pieces left on top the length of the trench. As the dramatic moment approaches for tossing the meat onto the fire, known as "t'rowing de buffalo," be sure that any unburned wood ends are removed and that the bed of coals is level. On goes the meat! It is quite a sight to see 20 to 30 steaks all cooking at once. The steak turners must stay alert to see that any burning around the edges is stopped by poking more coals and ashes up around them.

L.B. Sharp's favorite way to prepare the steaks for broiling was to sprinkle them with Worcestershire sauce; he then cut a raw onion in half and rubbed the flat surface over the meat. Although surface salting of meat before broiling tends to draw out the juices, I always do it. The terrific heat of the fire seals in the juices at once. Actually, any seasoning done beforehand leaves only the faintest of flavors on the cooked meat.

A Buffalo Steak Roast for a group of people is an unforgettable event, especially for those who have never seen one before. Even after many years, I am still a little awed when I "toss" (actually, place) a steak upon a bed of red-hot coals. Common sense says the meat should burn up—but it never does.

If you purchase hardwood charcoal or briquets you will probably have to use lighter fluid. Allow the fluid to burn off completely before cooking. The pieces of charcoal should be covered with wood ash, and a fierce heat should be generated before the steak is placed. Store-bought charcoal and briquets are inferior to a natural bed of glowing coals.

Can you cook hamburgers this way? The answer is no and yes—more care must be taken to have them come out right. Certainly, the thin, fatty burgers sold and served by the billions will probably burn up on the coals. If you buy *lean* ground beef and make the patties yourself, you can cook them in this way. The main trouble is that they often break apart when you turn them with a pancake turner. Some oatmeal mixed in helps to hold them together;

if you want, pat on some flour. The ground beef should be firmly compacted to no more than one inch in thickness, and the full thickness should extend to the circular edge. Try a cookie cutter or a tin can to cut patties from a firmed sheet of ground beef. With these modifications, hamburgers can be done (Fig. 28).

Baking

The reflector baker, preferably of the folding or "take-apart" kind, is the Northwoodsman's oven. With it he bakes delicious biscuits, cakes, pies, and cookies, and he can cook fish and even meat. Kephart recommended putting the food in a shallow pan (not shown) that fits on the reflector's shelf. For anything with juices, a pan (make one from foil) is needed. Even with biscuits a pan may be handy so that you can reverse front and back (use gloves!) if you are getting too much heat in front. In general, however, foil should not be taken into the woods. If you do take it, you must pack every scrap out. If buried, an animal may dig it up and eat it for the food still sticking to it. More than one woodland critter has died a slow and painful death in this way.

For baker cooking, the books say you should have a reflecting stone back or several green log sections piled up and secured by end stakes. Either arrangement reflects the heat so that the top of the food gets cooked in about the same time as the bottom. Although handy, you don't need them. Fig. 29 shows how to produce a wall of flame high enough to cook both top and bottom uniformly. You must

Fig. 28: "Buffalo" steak roast. 1) Steak pushed into hot coals. 2) Same, turned. The surface is gray, not burned. 3) Hamburgers in coals. 4) Hamburgers perfectly cooked.

have plenty of dry sticks to lean at a steep angle against the green "waugan" stick, big enough so it won't burn through until you have finished the baking. It takes some skill and experience to keep the fire burning just right. Before a stick burns to the point of dropping, another must be put on so the wall of flame won't have a hole in it. You'll soon learn from experience how far away from the flames to set the baker. The use of a reflector baker goes back at least to colonial times, when it was used in front of the indoor fireplace.

The other principal way of baking outdoors, is in a dutch oven, also an ancient and efficient way to cook. The heavy, thick-walled iron pot has a lid with a raised rim so that you can pile hot coals on top for better heating. Both pot and lid are preheated over the coals, then removed. Biscuits or what have you can be placed directly on the bottom, but to prevent possible sticking, it's better to put them in a pie tin kept off the bottom with three small pebbles. Put on the cover, set the pot back on the coals, and shovel a layer of the coals on top. Take a peek in about 10 minutes to see how things are going.

Dutch ovens are now available in aluminum, Fig. 29. Their lightness is an advantage, but the much heavier ones of cast iron hold heat longer and more uniformly. Even the lightest ovens hold no interest for backpackers, who must trim every possible ounce of weight, but they are excellent for fixed camps, or for the trail when you have pack animals to carry the burden. It's interesting to see how an old-timer brought up on a dutch oven has no use for a reflector baker, and perhaps vice-versa. M. Marshall, in his book *Cooking over Coals*, dismisses the reflector as being too variable and difficult to use. His excellent dutch-oven techniques and recipes span a lifetime of practice, and include delicious slow-cooked stews and roasts as well as breadstuffs.[4]

Having used a reflector many times in the past 50 years, I can recommend its modest cost and portability. And it allows you to watch the cooking process without lifting a lid. If you like outdoor (or indoor-fireplace) cooking, you can try both of these time-honored methods.

Sourdough Cookery

Anyone who has never eaten sourdough flapjacks or a slice of crusty sourdough bread has missed one of the great eating pleasures of mankind. Only recently I joined the club by getting a sour-

dough packet of starter from one of the Hickory Farms of Ohio counters found in many supermarkets. With the kit comes complete instructions, recipes, and a short history of sourdough cooking on the American frontier. Originally started from wild yeasts floating in the air, an extra good pot of sourdough was greatly treasured and handed down from one user to another. Years passed, and some of today's mixtures are said to have been started a half century ago.

When I got my pot going, I lifted a tiny speck of the dough, diluted it with water, and looked at it through a microscope. There were the untold millions of globular cells, some with side buds, all descendents of a wild yeast captured in some "sourdough's" pot so many years ago, perhaps in far-off Alaska! When you thrust your fingers into the mass of yeast-rising dough, knead it, and slap it around, you are sharing a soul-satisfying experience that goes back thousands of years. Do not be deterred by the sour smell of the pot. Besides the yeast cells, there is a newly discovered bacterium that produces acid.[5] This is neutralized by baking soda added to the dough mixture.

Firemaking with the Bow-drill

This is the most spectacular and significant of all woodcraft accomplishments. It fits in perfectly with the new widespread interest in primitive crafts. No one can really appreciate a match until he has mastered this ancient art, one that's perhaps 100,000 years old. I've made fire with a bow-drill hundreds of times before thousands of people, and I've read everything I could find out about it. Some of the instructions in the most recent books leave out certain essentials for success.

Only a few youngsters in each generation have the persistence and energy and can develop the skill to bring forth the magic fire from the trees of the forest. Most people have never seen it done, and have a hazy idea about it. After one of Ernest Thompson Seton's superlative lectures featuring the bow-drill, someone said, "I don't see why you go to all that trouble when you only have to scratch a match." Seton turned his piercing black eyes upon the questioner and said, smiling, "Ah! You are thinking only of the fire down there (pointing to the board). I'm also thinking of the fire up here," and he placed his hand over his heart.

The easiest way to get started is to buy a firemaking kit from a Boy Scout supply store. Current-

Fig. 29: Baking. 1) Vertical fire for reflector baking. 2) Dutch oven — coals underneath and on top of lid. 3) Cover removed from a Dutch oven — biscuits in pie tin.

ly, the fire board and drill are made from yucca, which yields a coal very quickly, but is found mostly in the arid Southwest. I'm enough of a purist to believe that local materials should be used, not something imported from 2,000 miles away. Every locality has one or more kinds of trees whose wood was used by the AmerIndians. These woods, soft and nonresinous, include the cedars, balsam fir, basswood, eastern cottonwood and other poplars, and even white pine, which, though resinous, some say is as good as any of the others. My favorite for a half-century has been eastern white cedar. City dwellers can go to a lumber yard to get a cedar post with as large a butt as possible, to minimize the number of knots. Take the post home and saw it into 14-inch lengths. (As a matter of principle, please use only hand tools.)

With an axe, split several sections into boards about three inches wide by ⅝-inch thick. You'll learn about grain in wood; if it is not straight, you can whittle lengthwise in one direction but not the other. You'll also need some 12-inch split pieces for drills; whittle them one inch square in cross-section. Then make them eight-sided by whittling each edge flat. Avoid any rounding. There must be eight good edges for the thong to grip. Whittle one end as shown in Fig. 31, No. 1; make the other end more tapered.

The bow is a stiff, naturally curved stick, 1½ inches bow to thong, about 26 inches long, and ¾ to one inch thick. The bow shown (Fig. 30) has a fork at the tip that makes it easy to attach the thong, but this isn't necessary. Near the other end of the bow is a hole (hidden in the photo by the hand) through which the adjustable end of the thong is passed and wrapped tightly around the bow.

The best thong is a yard-long piece of dry-tanned buckskin a full quarter-inch wide and ⅛-inch thick—it will last for years. Know any deer hunters? The thong in the kit is too thin, and tends to cut into a drill made from the softer woods. Note that it's twisted so that it can better grip the spindle (Fig. 30). "Indian-tan" belt lacing can be used, but it's slightly oily and may let the spindle slip just at the crucial moment. Thong slippage is an absolute no-no!

The final piece is the socket top, which you will grip when you start making fire. It should have a conical hole deep enough that the spinning drill won't suddenly jump out and spoil all your efforts. The one in the Scout kit is too small for comfort.

Cut a piece 4 × 2 × 1¼ inches; round the top edges, and carve shallow grooves to fit your fingers (Fig. 30). If the socket top is made of a hard wood (hickory, oak, hard maple, ironwood), or of a pine or hemlock knot, the hole can be drilled, or made with the tip of your knife. *Caution*: slant the knife toward you so it won't suddenly shut up and pinch or cut your forefinger. And don't hold the piece in your other hand—use a vise or other hold. Better yet, use a soft wood for this top piece and embed in it a frictionless socket piece. The Indian often used a small piece of soapstone for this purpose. The wooden top was beautifully carved to represent the Thunder Bird.[6] Keep the hole well greased with anything that will minimize friction.

For tinder there are many choices—finely shredded cedar bark, a field-mouse nest, white-pine needles, rope yarns that are teased apart, and fluffed-up rope yarns. This tinder and the fire board and drill must be bone-dry.

So now, after a lot of labor, you are ready to try it out. See Fig. 31, No. 1, and carve the hole with its center ¾-inch from the edge of the fire board. Study Fig. 30, and adjust the thong so that you think it will fit snugly around the drill. Hold the bow in one hand, and use the other hand to place the drill on the thong, facing the bow. Twist the drill into place. If the thong is too short, it won't work; too long, and it won't grip the spindle. Keep adjusting the thong length until it's just right.

When it is, and you get the drill in the pit, put on the socket top, and anchor the whole assembly by pressing your wrist tightly against your shin (Fig. 30). The drill must run true vertically, and should *never, never* wobble in the slightest. While getting to the vertical position, the drill will likely seem to have a mind of its own and will spring out. After some practice, you'll learn how to control it.

Now begin to make long, easy bow strokes, with moderate pressure on the top. Often on the very first stroke, the drill point will jump out, and the drill will escape again. Try cutting the pit a little deeper, or loosen the thong just a hair.

Now you have it all together, and the drill is merrily spinning. Just a few strokes and you get your first thrill—smoke is rising! Keep going until the hole looks like the one in Fig. 31, No. 2. Now lift out the drill. Stand the board on edge, and cut a clean ¾-inch notch whose tip is a hair short of the exact center of the hole. If it goes beyond the center, you'll probably get no fire. Why? I don't know.

Now you're ready for your first attempt. Check the tension on the thong. The tighter it is, the harder you have to work. But if it's not tight enough, it will slip. You can either place a hand-size mat of tinder under the notch, or catch the hoped-for coal on a thin chip (Fig. 31, No. 3 and No. 4) and transfer it to the tinder.

So here goes—long, steady bow strokes that increase in speed to your top capability, and slowly increase pressure on the socket. Fragrant clouds of cedar smoke billow upward, and a stream of hot, black powder, ground away by the spinning drill, begins to fill up the notch. Watch very carefully until you think plenty of smoke is actually coming from the powder in the notch, and not just from the drill and board. Stop and remove drill and bow. Now you can see better. Is smoke still rising? Tap the board gently if the powder sticks in the notch. Immediately fan the coal with one hand while removing the board with the other. The volume of smoke increases. If you wish to savor this moment of triumph, keep fanning for a few seconds more until you actually see the glowing center. Now make a shallow "bird's nest" of some tinder in the palm of your hand, and carefully tip the coal into its center. What you do next is of the greatest importance. Close your fingers so that the tinder makes a ball that fits snugly around the coal. Watch what you're doing. The tinder should surround and touch the coal, but if you squeeze too hard you'll crush it out. From now until the climax, do not move or disturb the tinder.

At this point in the fire-making process, there are two "schools": the "swingers" and the

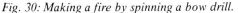

Fig. 30: Making a fire by spinning a bow drill.

"blowers." You can swing your arm back and forth to create a draft—or simply blow gently through the tinder. In either case, smoke increases, and so does the heat in your hand. Before it gets too hot, bring your other hand into play, holding the burning tinder between them—but keep blowing. Very soon you'll see a flash of flame. Stoop quickly and tuck the flaming tinder into the special place prepared for it in the Council Fire lay. If this is just a demonstration with no fire lay, hold the tinder aloft as it flames and hang on until the last second before letting the flaming mass fall to earth.

All this sounds easy, doesn't it? Well, it isn't, especially for the beginners. First of all, you may have difficulty in spinning the drill long enough to create the precious coal. Just as you near the crucial point, you begin to pant, your tired muscles go partly out of control, and the drill hops out of its socket. Or the thong, stretched by all the action, begins to slip, and the drill slows down. You then have to reduce pressure on the socket, and friction is no longer enough to ignite a coal. In either case, you must start all over again. Before doing so, look at the end of the drill. Is it developing a "shoulder" or overhang where it contacts the edge of the hole? Carefully whittle this off so that the diameters of the drill and hole are the same. You want all the friction in the blackened hole, not around the edge. Now tighten the thong once more, and try again.

This time everything works fine. The notch fills with black powder, and you're *sure* there must be a glowing coal in there somewhere. You carefully remove drill and board, and begin gentle fanning. Your soul is concentrated on that tiny wisp of smoke—but after a few seconds it diminishes, and soon there is no smoke at all. You sort of collapse inside, and the fire spirit intently watching you shrugs and fades away until another time.

Two things may have happened. First, you misjudged the amount of smoke. Perhaps a few more strokes with the bow would have meant success. Second, the tinder is not dry enough. Put it in the hot sun for an hour or so, or by the campfire. If you've used the same hole several times, it may be worn out—if it's more than two-thirds of the way through the board, you'd better start a new one. Continued use of the drill not only shortens it but also rounds the drill's original eight edges. Careful whittling restores them. When the drill gets too short for comfort, make a new one.

Repeated drilling puts unaccustomed stresses on body muscles. After several tries, I've seen many a teachers-college student, even Phys Ed majors, become "all wore out." Take your time—try again tomorrow.

Sometimes ear-splitting shrieks come from the whirling spindle and fire board. I've never really found the source. Maybe it's the wood nymph protesting.

A last admonition. Using this method to make fire in the dark is hardly possible—you can't see smoke rising from the notch. So at the Council Fire, if it's to be kindled at dusk, have an assistant with a penlight flashlight illuminate just the notch.

Council Fires

Long before the beginning of written history, our primitive ancestors used to assemble in the blackness of the night forest and dispel its gloom by kindling the magic fire. After a day of hunting and gathering, the members of a family would sit in a circle around the campfire. As they felt its warmth and watched the firelight play across each other's faces, something wonderful happened—something that could never be put into words. They felt a sense of oneness and security not found anywhere else.

When I think back to some of the hundreds of campfire groups I've known, I have no doubt that under the thin veneer of civilization, there is still that ancient something in human observers that always responds to a campfire's magic. Under its spell, differences in race, rank, religion, social position—all are muted. I've often thought that if negotiators for warring factions would meet around a campfire, their differences could be resolved more easily. (Actually, this has happened many times throughout history.)

Going back to the small family group: in time it grew, multiplied, and split into several new families. Each one moved away and set up its own camp. And then began the ages-long tradition of the occasional Council Fire. All the families came to discuss tribal affairs, to have contests of various kinds, do ritual dances, and tell stories that handed down the oral history of the tribe.

Every organized camp should have a council ring where all campers and staff gather once or twice a week. Ernest Thompson Seton, one of the greatest elders of our outdoor fraternity, wrote that at Council Fire, "we get at once the ancient spirit of the woods—the dramatic equalization of responsibility and of honor." Over the years, he personally

Fig. 31: 1) Conical knife-cut pit. 2) The first drilling to increase the size of pit. 3) Fire board notched to center of pit; glowing coal on chip pulled out to show notch. 4) Same—chip rests on fireboard. 5) Another coal on finely shredded cedar-bark tinder. 6) The fire.

helped 86 camps to construct council rings. Much of what follows is from his plans.

The selection of a site is of prime importance and may require considerable searching. Seton wrote, "It must be a dry, level, beautiful place in the woods," at least 40 feet across, and far enough from the main camp that none of its noises can be heard.[7] Waves from a large lake or the sea crashing on the shore would also be distracting. A council circle is a very special place, deep in the stillness of the woods. It is never entered or even approached except along the narrow winding trail that connects it to the main camp. The trail entrance should be left "blind" for a few feet, with a minimum of brush cut away. Small trees and shrubs that are removed must be cut level with the ground. The trail, although narrow, should be as free of obstacles as possible. Clip off branches on the sides and overhead. You may have 75 to 100 people walking along it single-file after dark. The whole spirit of the thing can be flawed if someone stumbles and lurches into the camper ahead, who in turn may throw the next off balance.[8]

When you think you've found *the* place to build the ring, stand at its center for a while and consider. Drive a stake. Loop one end of a cord over it. Measure 12 feet along the cord, and swing a 24-foot-diameter circle, marking it with stakes as you go around. How does it look? There should be no large trees that have to be removed, and no boulders. Small trees and shrubs are then severed at ground level, and all litter and humus in the ring are removed down to the mineral soil. Seton insisted on a hard-packed earth surface "as level as a tennis court."(!) He was thinking of a program featuring Indian dancing. To produce such an ideal "floor" in some camps I've visited would take a great deal of time and energy, and may be next to impossible. I greatly respect Indian dancing, especially in costume. But very memorable programs can be developed without it.

A circular plot having been cleared and levelled, the ring itself is formed by end-connected benches all the way around, except for a single entrance. The entrance faces exactly opposite the "council rock," which may be an eight-foot plank spiked to short, radially placed log sections. If there's a tree or boulder just outside the ring, place the council rock in front of it. Here sit the chiefs and other visitors or dignitaries. Starting at each end of the eight-footer, build the rest of the circle, using

shorter (five-foot) planks end-spiked to the partly flattened short logs to form a solid structure (Fig. 32). Of course, if large logs are available, five-foot log sections can form the ring. Such an arrangement will seat about 50 people (depending on their "beam"). You may build a larger circle, but if it exceeds 30 feet, the feeling of group togetherness lessens. The other solution is to build a second, raised ring around the first one. But this also reduces the feeling of oneness that a single circle promotes.

The success of a Council Fire depends first of all upon the fire itself—how it's kindled and tended. It should be built directly on the ground—not raised on an altar. I do not like the traditional four-square "log cabin," a three-foot-high structure. As it burns, it becomes unstable and collapses before the program is finished. Much better is a slant-stick (tipi) fire structure two feet high. It is an art to lay up, kindle, and most of all tend the fire so that it keeps giving maximum light until the program is nearly over. Then it slowly dies toward the end of the closing ceremony. The firemaker must be the very best you can find in camp.

An extra supply of sun-baked, bone-dry firewood, cut beforehand in appropriate lengths, is piled neatly beside the firesite and covered by a plastic sheet. There should be an oversupply of wood. Try having four times as much as you think you'll use. The fire may need tending every 10 minutes or so. Provide a low seat so that the firekeeper can sit close to the fire and replenish it as needed. Part of the art is to keep the fire just right without anyone else being aware of what you're doing.

And how will you light it to begin with? Certainly the bow-drill method of the AmerIndians, described earlier, is ideal. In every generation there are tens of thousands of people who've never seen this dramatic creation of a glowing coal, its placement in the tinder, the fragrant smoke rising, and then the first flash of flame. But it must be done well—otherwise, use a match. An alternative is the pioneer's flint and steel.

The greatest travesty I've ever seen in the lighting of a so-called Council Fire was at a counsellor's training session in a camp that shall remain nameless. The firemaker had not kept his wood dry and under cover. Why bother? He had just doused the five-foot-high log-cabin structure—wet from several hours of rain—with kerosene, "as usual." We smelled its stink as we silently approached the circle. When all were seated, there was some mumbo-jumbo from the firemaker directed to the Chief. Something about "bringing down fire from heaven." Suddenly, at the base of the pile there was a flash of fire, and up through the center of the log structure roared a tornado of flames. It might be called spectacular, but after a few minutes the kerosene burned off, and there was left only a smoking, stinking pile of wet wood. For once, the woodland spirits had foiled paleface chemistry! I was told that under the pile there was a dish of potassium chlorate. Over it was suspended a vial of sulfuric acid, triggered by a wire that passed through a buried pipe to the Chief's seat. A Moosewood Curse on any one of you who thinks well of the idea, and dares even to plan such a device for your council ring! That evening we sat out the program with the scant illumination of a few flashlights around the ring.

Counsellors must, of course, be already experienced, or briefed by the director or Chief on procedure. They will see that each of their campers has a blanket to wear Indian style. If camp blankets have been made "extinct" by sleeping bags, a sweater or jacket will have to do. Each camper should also have a dry, sound stick between six and eight inches long, and no larger than one inch in diameter. This is the camper's own contribution to the fire; by placing it there, he becomes linked in an almost mystical way to every one else in the circle. As firekeeper, I have watched many hundreds of campers add their brands to the fire. I have often

Fig. 32: Plan of council ring, from The Birchbark Roll of Woodcraft by Ernest Thompson Seton. (Courtesy A.S. Barnes, Publisher.)

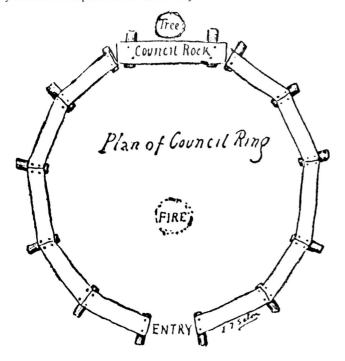

Omaha Prayer

Alice C. Fletcher—27th Ann. Rep. Bur. Eth., p. 130.

wished I knew their thoughts and feelings at that instant, but their expressions told me they would never forget their first Council Fire—or, for that matter, others that would come later.

Each counsellor should have a flashlight (to be used as little as possible), and, if the bugs are bad, some insect repellent for his group. The Council Fire experience can be ruined if everyone is being "chawed alive" by mosquitoes or punkies (no-see-ums).

The time to begin the ceremony is just before sunset, so that it will be easy to follow the special trail from the assembly point through the woods to the council ring. The Chief, any visitors, and the firemaker may precede the campers by a few minutes. The AmerIndians also assigned two guards or "dog-soldiers" to sit, one on each side, at the entrance. They were to prevent anyone who didn't belong from entering the circle.

When all have promptly assembled at the trail's beginning, a counsellor may face toward the council ring and give an appropriate call—that of the barred owl is a good one (*Who-who, who-who, who-who, who-whoah*). This is answered from the council rock (a tom-tom is appropriate), and then the groups start along the trail in single-file. When they reach the entrance, the first counsellor leads his campers to the right, the second to the left, and so on until both halves of the ring are about equally filled. Everyone remains standing silently until the Chief gives a word or a gesture to be seated.

Now is the time for the Chief to set the tone for the whole program, ceremony, ritual, or whatever he wishes to call it. His few words said seriously, but not too much so, must come from the heart. This introduction to council is most important; it should always be well-thought-out beforehand. When finished, he may turn to the firemaker and say, "Now kindle our Council Fire." If this is the first fire of the camping period, the firemaker should explain simply what he is about to do. Too many people think that one lights a fire just by "rubbing two sticks together"! The firemaker might also relate this Council Fire to the countless others going back in time to man's ancient discovery of fire—still the most important discovery he has made.

After the fire is burning brightly, each group in turn approaches the fire, and one at a time the campers place their sticks upon it. It's always interesting to see how and where each camper does this. At first, it makes little difference to the fire-keeper just where the sticks are placed, but soon he may see that some direction is needed. He can point silently to where he'd like each group's contributions. As the sticks pile up, the fire burns ever more brightly. Each group backs away to its place in the circle. At no time do you ever turn your back to the fire. The last group to approach the fire is the group from the council rock itself. The Chief adds the last stick, and when all have retired to their places, he may say, "This Council Fire is now open."

At this point, there's been enough solemnity for a while, and the gathering should be livened up. Some of the AmerIndian's "challenges" are good. A camper may challenge anyone (except those on the council rock) to a talkfest. The two contestants stand facing each other near the center of the ring, and at "Go" from a counsellor-referee, they both start talking to each other. To win, you must talk, without stopping, for two minutes on the referee's watch. It's not easy with the challenger trying to talk you down. Usually the referee's decision is accepted, but if it's a close thing, he can put it to a vote. The winner may then challenge someone else. This can go on for three or four rounds, but of course it should not be long enough for the group to start losing interest—a cardinal principle in recreation education.

Another good game is the "frozen face" contest. The challenger picks his victim and tries to make him laugh or even smile. As before, they stand facing each other. The challenger must not touch his opponent, but he can do about anything else—tell funny stories, make faces, ask leading questions, etc. This is excellent training in self-control, and lots of fun for the spectators.

About now is a good time for songs. I've been privileged to lead some of the finest group singing I've ever heard, out in the night forest around a campfire. Many books of songs are available. In a resident camp, the groups should be encouraged to write their own songs of the outdoors, and about camp happenings. Through the years, a camp can build up a priceless collection of such songs—and thus evolve traditions unique to that camp.

If you have a counsellor interested and expert in teaching Indian dancing, you have a pearl of great price. Costumes can be made by the campers and saved from one year to the next.

These activities will have kept the group at a high pitch of emotional involvement, and now it's time for a change of pace. Nature reports are invited by the Chief, who may call upon his counsellors for help with information. Campers are encouraged to be constantly observant and to bring in questions or comments about what they've seen, heard, or otherwise experienced, to the council ring. With a new group, you may have had to arrange with two or three campers beforehand in getting the thing started. If the counsellor can get a camper to answer his own question by asking him several others, excellent—this is ideal. But often no one knows the answer, and even if one does, it may be better to give only part of the story and refer the camper to a book in the camp library. Remember, as you listen to these questions and reports, that the ecology of the surrounding mysterious forest still has uncounted secrets.

It takes skill to preside over these nature reports—some will be very funny, some rather dull, others so twisted up that it's difficult to unravel them. In any case, the dignity of the individual must be preserved. He must not be made fun of—too much!

At one evening campfire at the Hudson, Ohio, Nature Guide School, I was firemaker and song leader. The group included both students (mostly schoolteachers) and a lively bunch of town school kids. After nature reports, Chief Cap'n Bill Vinal suggested I call in a screech owl (certainly a poor name for this little owl; the southern name "shivering owl" is much better). His tone of voice suggested that there was no doubt that I could get one of these winged critters to come on in! He hadn't briefed me beforehand, and I felt no certainty at all that I could perform such a stunt. Anyway, I asked for absolute silence, and then began whistling the quavering call. After about four repetitions, I heard a murmur from the campers and saw a hand pointing up. There on a tree limb, barely visible in the flickering firelight, sat a little screech owl. And suddenly, on silent wings, came another. I kept whistling. Finally there were *five* of them perched on various trees surrounding the campfire circle. We were all enthralled—especially the kids. Needless to say, I've never had such an experience again —one owl perhaps, but never five![9]

After the nature reports and discussions, a few more songs are appropriate, this time of a quieter sort as the Council Fire program winds down toward its conclusion. Then comes the last, and perhaps the most important, feature of the evening—the story. I can do no better than to recommend Seton's "Trail and Campfire Stories".[10] Pre-

ceding the 20 stories is a sensitive analysis of his storytelling techniques and some extremely useful hints by his wife Julia M. Seton, who watched his matchless performances for many years. Even one of his bitterest critics, John Burroughs, finished one of his tirades with: "I must admit that Seton is the greatest raconteur in America."

Mrs. Seton wrote: "Never, never read a story. There is no magnetism, no contact of personalities, during reading."[11] Go over a story until it's yours. Tell it in your own words. If you are the camp director-Chief, the story is your great opportunity at the Council Fire.

Following the story, the Chief may say, "Our Council Fire burns low." An appropriate ending is the singing of the Omaha Tribal Prayer:

Wah-kahn-dah, Day-doo: Wah-pah-dee, nah-tone-nay.

(Repeat)
"Father, a needy one stands before you;
I the singer am he."

There are several versions. This one seems to be the easiest to teach. Note that the leader must start on a fairly high note, or at the end he'll have everyone down in the "sub-basement." All stand with their arms raised, and lower them slowly so that at the last note they are down, and the head is inclined in a prayerful position.

If you prefer, all campers may join hands and sing "Taps."

Day is done, gone the Sun,
From the lake, from the hills, from the sky,
All is well, safely rest, God is nigh.

Everyone leaves silently, in the reverse order of their entering—those on the council rock last. When all have gone, and the darkened forest is silent, the firemaker carefully soaks with water the dying embers of another memorable Council Fire, and departs carrying memories that only he can have.

A contribution from one who knew campfire magic:

"There is an impalpable, invisible, softly stepping delight in the campfire which escapes analysis. Enumerate all its charms, and still there is something not in your catalogue. There are paths of light which it cuts through the darkness; there are elfish forms winking and twisting their faces in the glowing ash-veiled embers; there are black dragons' heads with red eyes, and jaws grinning to show their fiery teeth; the pines whisper to the silence; the sentinel trees seem to advance and retire. At night, when the torch is applied to the wealth of accumulated fuel, they are trees no longer. They leave their places and come out of the darkness to join our company. They say not a word, and yet not even to man is given such a variety of character and so much of the mystery of the spiritual world.

"The evening campfire burns low. One by one the brands have dissolved into coals, and one by one the little circle has retired into the cabins and gone to sleep. I take from a pile of the skeleton of a dead pine one of its huge resinous bones and cast it on the coals. The surrounding trees have all retired into the silent darkness to repose from the toils of the stormy day—now with its wrestling winds also gone into the darkness of the past. Immediately the yellow flames shoot up high, and the trees step out of the darkness on silent feet, with a surprised expression, as if to say, as they look down upon me, 'Why, we did not expect you to call for us again.' And there they stand waiting, with the stars glittering in their tangled hair." –*Dr. Wm. C. Gray, 1830-1901 (from his book,* Campfire Musings, *1894)*

FIRE

1. Page 62—Horace Kephart, *Camping and Woodcraft.* Riverside NJ: Macmillan, 1972.

2. Page 64—Frances Densmore, *How Indians Use Wild Plants for Food, Medicine, and Crafts.* New York: Dover, 1974.

3. Page 65—Nessmuk (G.W. Sears), *Woodcraft.* New York: Dover, 1963.

4. Page 68—Mel Marshall, *Cooking Over Coals.* New York: Winchester Press, 1971.

5. Page 68—For more about the acid-producing bacterium, see *Scientific American* magazine, November 1973.

6. Page 70—For an excellent Chippewa story of the Thunder Bird, See Densmore.

7. Page 74—Julia Moss Seton, *By a Thousand Fires.* Garden City, NY: Doubleday, 1967.

8. Page 74—For additional details on council fire sites, see Bernard Mason, *Woodcraft and Camping.* New York: Dover, 1974.

9. Page 77—Owl story from "Wings at the Campfire," *Nature Study Journal of Environmental Education and Interpretation,* Winter 1974-75, page 9. The entire number is a series of tributes by more than 100 former students and colleagues to Dr. William G. "Cap'n Bill" Vinal.

10. Page 77—Ernest Thompson Seton, *Trail and Camp Fire Stories,* Melrose Park, IL: Boy Scouts of America.

11. Page 77—Julia Moss Seton, *By a Thousand Fires.*

FROM HERE TO THERE

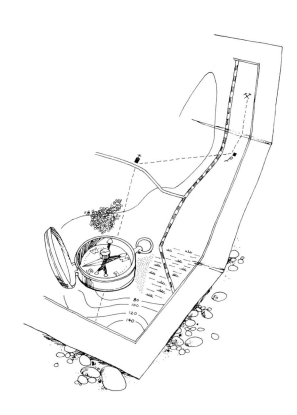

The Compass

Man has never been content to stay in the same place very long; he is constantly moving about from "here" to "there." To get from here to there, you need to know *direction* and *distance*. Also, in planning, it is good to know your speed; from this you can tell the *time* it may take to reach your destination.

People have no inborn sense of direction. Many times in the woods, I've said suddenly to a new group, "Point north!" Hands usually shot out in many different directions: east, west, south, north, and points in between. With no wind or sun to feel on the body and no noises to hear, a blindfolded person trying to walk in a straight line on level ground actually makes a curved path. Try it some time in the middle of a big field or lawn, and have

someone watch you; or with a light snow cover, shut your eyes and walk 50 paces. Look behind. You have trod a smooth curve. Now try again, leaning a little the other way. This time the curved track is reversed. You just can't walk in a straight line. Is it because one leg is a bit shorter than the other? Does right-handedness or left-handedness have any effect? The same thing happens when you shut your eyes and try to paddle a canoe on a calm lake.

Long before the compass appeared, men were sailing the oceans, using seasonal prevailing winds, the sun, and the stars to guide them. On land, having determined the way to go, you can do fairly well for an hour or so by keeping your path at about the same angle to the sun. Although the sun "rises in the east and sets in the west," it actually does so only on two days each year—the spring and fall equinox, about March 21 and September 22. These days contain approximately 12 hours of daylight and 12 hours of darkness over the whole earth from pole to pole. After March 21, the sun rises and sets farther and farther north in the northern hemisphere from true east and west until the summer solstice, about June 21, the longest day of the year. Then it "travels south" until, on September 22, it again rises in the east and sets in the west. Beyond that date, the sun rises and sets farther and farther south until December 22, the winter solstice, the shortest day (and longest night) of the year. Our ancient ancesters were filled with dread as this day approached. Would the sun never stop its retreat? All sorts of sacrifices and incantations were made, and they worked: the sun always stopped and began to return, warming the frozen land once more. All of this we had almost forgotten, living in our artificially lighted and warmed or cooled homes. But as long as the energy crisis lasts, the seasons will again become very real. Seasonal changes have always governed those who live in the forest, or travel, or make their living from the land.

You can get your approximate bearings in most of the northern hemisphere by pointing the hour hand of your watch (standard time—better yet, local time) at the sun; halfway from the hour hand to 12 noon on the watch face is south. To avoid looking at the sun, hold a straight, two-inch-long, slender weed stem or twig vertically so that the lower end touches the watch rim beyond the tip of the hour hand. Turn the watch until the shadow lies along the hour hand.

At night you can rely on that great gift, the

north star. We who live in the northern hemisphere may forget that south of the equator there is no such virtually unmoving beacon to guide the traveler. (Actually the north star moves in a very small circle, but this can be disregarded by ordinary travelers.) It does more than show true north; if you can measure the angle between the horizon and the star, you will also have your approximate position in degrees north latitude, which can be converted into miles north of the equator. On the equator (0° latitude), the north star is practically invisible. As you travel farther and farther north, the star seems to climb higher until it is almost directly overhead at the north pole—hence its name, Polaris or pole star. What a remarkable coincidence that there should be such a useful star!

Scattered around the world are deposits of magnetic iron ore (magnetite), one form of which, lodestone, has polarity. If you balance a bit of it on a wood chip, the ore will turn so that one end points to magnetic north. The ancient Chinese, Arabs, Greeks, and others have all been credited with discovering this phenomenon. The only hard fact we have is that the compass was in use by early navigators some time in the 12th and 13th centuries. It had been found that a steel needle stroked with a piece of lodestone became magnetized. When the needle was carefully balanced with a jewelled bearing set upon a pivot so that it could swing freely, it was an excellent direction indicator.

The literature on magnetism is enormous, but the phenomenon is still something of a mystery. Motors, dynamos, and countless other devices depend upon this force. The earth itself is a kind of gigantic magnet. Some 1,400 miles south of the geographic north pole is the north magnetic pole. The south magnetic pole is in Antarctica, and between these two poles are irregularly curving invisible lines of magnetic force. One of these lines bears southward from the north magnetic pole through Canada, passes near Chicago, and follows a southeasterly course that finally runs the length of Florida into the Atlantic Ocean. If you live along this line, known as the *agonic* line, your compass needle points true north. As you move farther and farther east, the needle points more and more to the west, until in Maine the angle between true north and magnetic north is about 20°. Geographers and school teachers would say this is 20° W *declination;* sea and air navigators call it *variation.* As you may guess, when you travel west from the line of 0°

variation, the compass needle points more and more to the east of true north; on the west coast at Vancouver, the variation is about 25° E. How to take care of this error is explained in the section on using maps.

Although you should always have faith in your compass, you must also know what things may cause it to deviate from pointing to magnetic north. Any objects made of steel, iron, or nickel, if large enough or near enough to the compass, will cause the needle to move. Experiment with your closed pocket knife. Bring one end toward the compass. How close must it be to move the needle? Does the north-pointing end move toward or away from the knife? If toward, try reversing the knife end for end. Now does the needle end move away from the knife? Try holding the knife horizontally over the compass. Lower the knife until the needle moves. Slowly turn the knife in a circle. What happens? All these effects are usually greater with carbon-steel blades; stainless steel is often much less magnetic.

In the field, what other things may affect the compass? Do you have a steel belt buckle? Try moving the compass from about a foot away from you toward the buckle. At how many inches is the effect so small you can disregard it? Of course, such objects as guns, flashlights, wire fences, axes, and saws must be checked out. And never try to use a compass within 200 feet of a high-tension power line! Many a hiker-photographer carries an electronic exposure meter strung around his neck or in his breast pocket. If you have one of these meters, just see what happens to the compass needle when you move the meter toward it (Fig. 33, No. 1). At 10 inches, the needle may deviate 10°. Turn the meter end for end, and the deviation will probably be about the same in the reverse direction. When the meter and compass are held close together, you may get an error of 20° to 45°! Suppose, not knowing about this, you tried to use your compass with the meter dangling a few inches above it: what then?

Even a camera may cause deviation when held close. Although the camera body is probably nonmagnetic, it may contain film spools and other parts made of steel, as well as a built-in exposure meter. Experiment and find out what happens. Finally, there are a few places in this great land where beds of magnetic iron ore are found. You can find out about these from local geologists or the U.S. Geological Survey.[1] The effect of these beds would be too insignificant to mention, but you may

*Fig. 33: The compass. 1) Exposure meter affects needle on compass.
2) A simple needle compass—end of needle pointing to magnetic
north is blue. 3) Needle in this compass is attached underneath to
compass card, which shows directions.*

have heard of it and have an exaggerated idea of its importance. As a general principle, always *trust your compass.*

Fig. 33, No. 2 and No. 3, show, enlarged, two kinds of simple compasses. In the first, both ends of the needle look the same except that the north-pointing end is bluish. If you have such a compass, turn it over and scratch on the back "Blue=North." Many a camper or hunter lost on a cloudy day has sworn that south was north because he couldn't remember which needle end was which. In the second kind of compass, you see no needle at all. It is attached underneath to the *compass card,* which shows directions.

To use the compass with the visible needle, you must always turn the compass until the north-pointing end of the needle lies directly over north on the compass card. (Since in magnetism opposite poles attract, the north-pointing end of a compass needle is actually the south end.) The card may show the cardinal points—N, E, S, and W; and also the intercardinals—NE, SE, SW, and NW. But modern compasses show a full 360° circle, with north being designated by either 0° or 360°.

Have you ever wondered why 360 was chosen as the number of divisions in a circle? Try dividing all numbers from one to 10 into 360. The one that won't go is seven, the "magical" number. According to a 1909 dictionary, the Babylonians seem to have chosen the division some time around 2000 to 3000 B.C. The dictionary surmises that "the degree was one of the daily steps of the sun on its annual path around the sky among the stars." Doubtless the Babylonians knew that the year was longer than 360 days, but they could not overlook the unique mathematical properties of the number.

Now then, how does one use a compass to go from here to there? Shrink yourself to the size of a small ant, and clamber to the center of the compass. Look around. What do you see? If you extend the degree marks in to the center, you suddenly realize that you are sitting in the middle of a kind of huge traffic circle with 360 "streets" running out from it. Face N and there is 0 street; to go NE it would be 45th street; E, 90th street, and so on all around the circle to 360th (0) street. You should always remember the four cardinal points, 0, 90, 180, and 270 as being N, E, S, and W.

You may hear the word "azimuth." Someone may say, "My azimuth is 185." All that means is that he's going out 185th street, or a little west of south.

Azimuth comes from the Arabic and means "the way," or "the way to go." Remember, then, that the center of the compass is always the starting point in going from here to there. The larger the dial of the compass, the more accurate the sighting will be. You should think of the line extending backward from the center to the reverse "street" number, touching the rim on the opposite side. This doubles the length and the accuracy of your sighting across the compass.

Since 1946, when I obtained my first Silva compass, I have used no other kind. To quote from "Silva Directions," (Silva, Inc., La Porte, Indiana), "This invention turned out to be the first substantial improvement in compass construction in several hundred years!" The genius of its Swedish inventor, Gunnar Tillander, was to mount a compass on a rectangular transparent plate that served as a protractor. Tillander's friends, the Kjellström brothers, began manufacturing the new compass.[2] The news spread like wildfire, and the factory currently turns out more than a million compasses a year. It is the official compass of the Boy Scouts and Girl Scouts and is used by countless others throughout the world.

For many years, the basic Silva compass was the "dry" model (Fig. 33, No. 1). It might take 10 seconds or so for the quivering needle to come to rest. As this was written, a new liquid-filled model was being introduced (Fig. 34). The liquid-filled compass needle comes to rest very quickly. It is hoped that "Red End North" will be printed inside this and all other models.

Assuming that the "direction of travel" arrow is pointing away from you (Fig. 34) in the direction you wish to go, you now turn the circular housing until the magnetic needle lies directly over the outlined or orienting arrow below. In the case shown, you turn the housing to the right (clockwise) and your degree reading or azimuth is 260, or 10° south of west. Now sight over the center of the "traffic circle" and out along the travel arrow to some landmark in the distance. Put the compass in your pocket or other safe place and walk to the landmark. Depending upon the kind of country, this mark may be as close as 20 feet (a tree in thick underbrush) or as far away as 20 miles (a mountain peak in open country). Whenever you cannot see your landmark, stop, take out your compass, and see that it is still set on 260. It is unlikely, but possible, that the housing has turned. Now, with the travel arrow pointing away from you, hold the compass level, and turn your body until the magnetic needle again lies over the orienting arrow as already described. This must always be done before determining a direction. Arriving at your tree, go halfway around it, orient the compass, pick another tree up ahead, and so keep going.

You may come to a very dense thicket or other obstruction. In this case, after orienting the compass, make a turn, sight along the base of the compass, which is 90° from your direction of travel line, and proceed until clear of the obstruction. Orient again and proceed along your 260° course until clear; then orient, make a reverse right-angle turn, and return to your original track. Orient and go ahead on your chosen course. At no time do you touch the housing to change the setting. If the right-angle offsets are more than 20 feet or so, you should pace the distances out and back. In this case, when you get back on line, a back bearing may be taken:

just turn the compass end for end so the direction of travel arrow points toward you, and sight along it backward. You should be looking at your last landmark. Any time you want to retrace your course to your starting point, this is the simplest way to do it. For slightly greater accuracy, add 180° to 260° and reset the housing to this new figure. $180 + 260 = 440$; $440 - 360 = 80°$, or in this case more simply $260 - 180 = 80°$ (10° north of east), your direction back home.[3]

Sometimes it's not convenient or even necessary to follow a compass course as described. In some cases you can use a baseline, which might be a road, stream, powerline, or fence that runs fairly straight for a mile or two away from your starting point. Suppose, for simplicity, that the baseline runs north and south. Now you can take off toward the east and wander around hunting or exploring for an hour or two without keeping track of direction at all. Then you just get out your compass and go west

Fig. 34: The Silva compass. (Photo by Silva Co.)

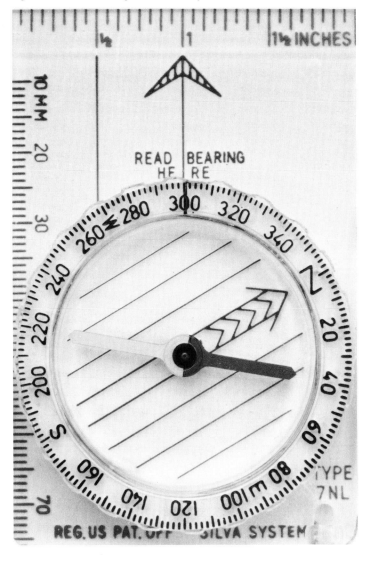

knowing that you'll reach the baseline. Simple and foolproof, isn't it?

Well, not quite. When you get there, you say to yourself, "Which way is my car?" You don't know. With all that walking around, it might be either north or south along the baseline. Before you ever use this device, you have to walk along the entire length of the baseline and memorize its landmarks. Or, much more simply, mark a small arrow every hundred yards or so on a rock or tree pointing toward car or camp. Get from any lumber-supply yard a stick of yellow and of blue lumber crayon ("keel" to the lumberman). Marks made with it have slight environmental impact and weather away within a few weeks or months. Some have suggested that toilet paper be used for temporary markers, but the idea doesn't appeal to me. It may blow away within a few minutes. You'll find a more detailed description of the baseline method in Kephart's *Camping and Woodcraft*, the first comprehensive volume on the subject written by one of the master woodsmen of all time.[4] Kephart suggested blazing trees along a compass line when no other baseline is available. Our wildernesses are now so overrun that his practice is taboo! There is, of course, a relationship between the length of the baseline and the distance or time you can safely stray away from it. In returning, you might find that you have travelled too far north or south of your last markers and have overrun one end or the other. You should take account of the kind of country to determine how long you think the baseline should be.

Beginners with a compass should practice taking bearings and pacing a magnetic course before starting out through the trackless forest. Stand in one place and take bearings on distant or nearby objects until you get the feel of the thing. Be sure to take many sightings from E through S to W. Most illustrations in books seem to prefer an example of a bearing in the northeast quadrant. When you set your compass for 170° and turn your body until the north-pointing end of the needle lies over the head of the orienting arrow, the arrow and needle will of course be aimed nearly at you. Until you get used to this position, you may feel peculiar about it. I've seen more than one novice with the magnetic needle reversed! The direction of an object from you is its *bearing*. If you start walking toward it, you are then treading a *course* or track of the same azimuth. If you ever expect to pilot a boat, it's important that you remember the difference between bearing and course.

One of the land surveyor's problems is to lay out a rectangular piece of ground and stake the four corners. Without bothering to mark the corners, this is a challenging project for you. Kjellström suggests making it more interesting by placing a coin on the ground as a starting point. Choose a direction, and pace off 100 feet (one pace equals two steps). Add 90° to your course direction, and pace the second 100-foot leg. Repeat twice more, and at the end of the last 100 feet, there should be your coin![5] To find the length of your pace, drive in a stake and accurately measure a straight 100-foot line (steel tape works best). Mark the other end with a stake. Now, using your normal easy walking gait, pace the distance several times and average the figures. Start with the right foot, and count each time the left foot strikes the ground. For many adults, a pace is between 4.7 and 5.0 feet. Five is handy: 20 paces equals 100 feet. The relation between a pace and a mile is quite interesting. The mile derives from *mille passus*, or 1,000 paces of the Roman soldier. The average soldier's pace was 4.86 feet; thus the Roman mile was 4,860 feet.

Your pace is a variable thing, often longer downhill, shorter uphill, longer on open ground, and shorter in the woods, especially if the path is brushy. Pacing, however, is much better than not measuring at all, as we shall see when we travel by map. When you measure your pace, do so alone. Two or more people walking influence each other's stride.

Although everyone taking to the woods should be expert with the compass, there are many areas, especially in western North America, where one may travel without using it very often. When a famous hiker says that in all the years he has travelled the wilderness he has used his compass only twice, I can guess that he has hiked in the magnificent semiopen forests of the Sierra Nevada or the Rocky Mountains; there and in many other places, one can see a long way ahead, and perhaps keep a mountain landmark in sight for half a day or more. In the rainforests of the Pacific Northwest and in vast areas in Canada and the eastern and southern United States, the forest is so dense that in many places you cannot see more than 50 feet in any direction. There you never set foot off a road or well-known trail without your compass. Old woodsmen who know their home range like the back of their hand may not use one. But one cloudy day, I

Fig. 35: Map dates and scales.

Mapped, edited, and published by the Geological Survey
Control by USGS and USC&GS
Topography from planetable surveys 1886, 1908 and 1933
Culture revised from aerial photographs taken 1953
Field check 1955-1956
Selected hydrographic data compiled from USC&GS surveys (1959)

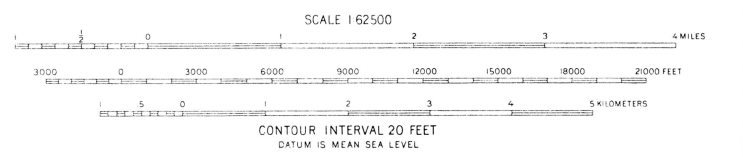

SCALE 1·62500

CONTOUR INTERVAL 20 FEET
DATUM IS MEAN SEA LEVEL

Fig. 36: Side view and contour map of an area. (Courtesy U.S. Geological Survey.)

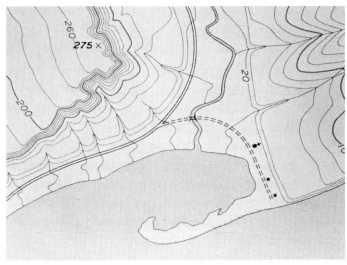

was with an old-timer who was just as lost as I was—just a piece of carelessness, really. We weren't bothering to use a compass!

Maps

When you first unroll that brand-new map and begin to study it, there are three things to look for at once: the date, the Date, and the DATE. One day I was walking along a back-country dirt road with several observant camp counsellors. One said, "The map shows a house just up ahead on the right, but I don't see it." A few hundred feet farther, and there it was: but it was a house no longer—only a cellar hole with three-inch trees growing out of it.

"But how can this be? We just got this map from the government."

I said, "Look at the date." The map had been surveyed 40 years before we set out to use it. Fig. 35 shows that there may be more than one date on the map, especially if it represents a famous area like Crater Lake National Park, Oregon, first surveyed before the turn of the century. The latest field-check date is also found under the map name in the lower right-hand corner.[6]

After you've found the date or dates, you'll want to know how big an area the map represents. On U.S. Geological Survey maps, the scale may be shown as 1:62,500. This means that one unit (inch, foot, centimeter, meter, or any other) on the map equals 62,500 of the same units on the land. 62,500 inches equal a little less than a mile, but walking distance is always more than that scaled from a map (which measures as the crow flies)—sometimes much more! A great many of the earlier quadrangles used the 1:62,500 scale, but now more and more of them are coming out at 1:24,000—one inch equals about 2,000 feet. Of course, much greater detail is shown by the new maps drawn at this larger scale. If you have the quandrangle names for old maps, the U.S.G.S. will furnish copies at $1 each. You can spend many pleasant hours comparing the features of an old map with those of a new one covering the same locality. Then you can go exploring to see what may have changed since the newest map was published.

Most immediate changes have to do with man's impact on the land—new roads, dams, and power lines. But nature too is constantly changing the face of the land in many ways. Some changes take years or centuries; others, especially those in the courses of streams and rivers, may occur after a single spring freshet. I recall canoeing down a narrow New Hampshire stream that, according to the map, ran directly into a small pond. But as we approached it, we could see that the stream would enter way over on the pond's left side. Did the map-maker goof those many years ago, or had the stream actually changed its course? We paddled over to the head of the pond and there, still faintly visible and nearly filled with bog shrubs, was the old channel.

Underneath the numerical map scale (Fig. 35) are bar scales in miles, feet, and kilometers. Most of the time you'll use the miles scale—you'll find that you will never forget that a map distance is less than the travelled distance. An exception is if you are crossing a perfectly level plain and the surface is such that you can travel in a straight line toward a distant landmark.

Most terrain, however, isn't nearly so regular. So now we come to the "ups and downs," and how they are shown on a "topo" map. Fig. 36 used to be shown on the back of U.S.G.S. maps and has been reprinted in many a book. It represents a river valley, with some steep slopes on the left and more gentle ones on the right. The shape of the land on the map below is shown by brown contour lines. After you get used to interpreting them, they give you a three-dimensional effect as though you were hovering in a helicopter directly over any mapped point. Contour lines are like debris lines on a beach, as if the ocean were to rise in stages, in this case 20 feet. Each stage is called the *contour interval.*

Look carefully at the shore-line on the map. This may be called the zero contour line. Now, starting at the lower left, follow the first contour line around until it disappears at the top of the map and then reappears on the other side of the river. Here it is labelled "20", which you knew already. Look at the river. We know that from the top of the map to the river's mouth, it drops less than 20 feet. Why? Because the 20-foot contour line does not cross it. It does cross somewhere upriver, but how much farther up we don't know. We can guess that this is a placid river, good for easy canoeing, but we can't be sure. There is no map scale. The roads, church, and houses are symbols, and are not to scale. The canoeist has no way of knowing whether the river drops gradually. It looks as though it does, but in actuality there might be a 10 to 15-foot drop, probably near the top of the map, followed by slow water down to the bay.

Look again at the side view of the land, and

see how each feature is shown by successive contour lines on the map. It's evident that the four distant hills are beyond the top border of the map. You can see that the closer the contour lines are to each other, the steeper is the slope. Just above the church, the land rises sharply; then there is a more gentle slope between the 40-foot and 60-foot contour lines. But again, never forget that between any two such lines there may be all sorts of ups and downs that do not quite equal the contour interval. After crossing that 40-foot contour line on the way up, you might go down 10 feet or so, walk on level ground for a ways and then find yourself facing a 15-foot cliff! In some cases, such outstanding features may be shown on the map by dotted or dashed lines, but don't count on it. One more example: the "flat" peninsula enclosing the bay. Maybe the land *is* flat,

but there could be sand dunes 19 feet high.

None of the above comments is intended to detract in any way from the high quality of these superb maps, which require enormous amounts of time and great skill to produce. However, you should know their limitations. In relatively flat country, the contour interval may be but five feet. Were it 20 feet, or even 10 feet, there might not be any contour lines at all! Maps of hilly country usually show an interval of 20 feet, and in mountainous regions the interval is often 80 or 100 feet. You can see that the greater the contour interval, the more chance there is of finding topographical surprises between one imaginary line and the next one above or below it.

Now look carefully at the stream valleys in the top picture, and how they're shown on the map below. When a contour line crosses a stream it forms

Fig. 37: Map oriented by a magnetic meridian and compass. The protractor is used to measure 11° west variation from a five-minute true meridian. The magnetic arrow on a map may be in error as much as 2°. Here the two magnetic meridians are parallel for all practical purposes.

what some writers call an "arrowhead" pointing toward the stream's source. This is because the stream is lower than the hill surrounding it. To see why this is so (it confuses many beginners), cut a potato in half and place it flat side down in a baking pan. Carve a valley down your potato "hill." You can then fill the pan with water in set stages of, say, half an inch. At each rise, there is a new contour line.

By now no one needs to tell you that all points on a contour line are the same vertical distance above sea level. If you could follow such a line, you'd go neither up nor down. This is why man, when he had a choice, settled in such wide, gently sloping river valleys as the one shown. Notice that the bayside road on the left follows just below the 20-foot contour line and doesn't cross it until both are near the top of the map.

Having learned something about contour lines, does it occur to you that if you map-scale the distance from the bay straight to the top of "275X," this will not be the actual distance from bay to hilltop? All distances measured on these topo maps are *horizontal* distances. In going up or down gentle slopes, the measured distance is not much less than the actual one. If the terrain rises at a 30° angle to the horizontal, one measured mile on the map equals about 1.15 miles on the land; but on a 45° slope, one map mile equals 1.4 to be climbed. Something to consider.

You should take steps to prepare a map for field use. If the parallels and meridians are not actually shown, they will be indicated by tick marks along the margins. Draw them in with a straightedge. You now will usually have nine sections. With a large protractor having a six-inch or more base, carefully lay off from a true meridian the stated magnetic variation (declination) on the map, and draw a magnetic north-south line. The reason for not just projecting the printed magnetic arrow upward is that it may be in error as much as two degrees and is not intended for precise use. Fig. 37 shows the compass edge along a magnetic meridian.

Cut around the map margin, but save the border with its important information. Lay down on a spread-out newspaper a smooth piece of cheesecloth a little larger than the map. Cut along the top parallel and then along the two meridians. Now you have the top third of the map in three pieces. Using a waterproof household cement (Duco or equivalent), carefully adhere the three pieces to the cheesecloth, spacing them not more than ⅛-inch apart. Continue

until you have mounted the whole map. As the cement dries, see that the cement has not oozed through the cheesecloth and stuck it to the newspaper.

When the map is thoroughly dry, cut out the bar scale and cement it along the vertical edge of a section. The quadrangle name, the part that shows the direction of north, and other possibly useful information can be adhered to the back of the map. By mounting the map in this way, you can fold it so that any section is visible. Make a stiff plastic envelope, and insert the folded map. Nothing is more of a nuisance on a hike than a rolled-up map; even when folded, it's still not handy. It's difficult to lay flat, it soon wears out along the folds, and a strong wind makes a plaything of it.

To get from here to there, you now have a compass and map—a perfect combination. Of course, you could orient the map by standing on a straight road and turning the map until the depicted road is parallel to the real one. Be sure you know where north is. Otherwise, you might get the map reversed; this has been done too! In most cases, you'll use your Silva compass. Fig. 37 shows how this has been done. Unfold the map and spread it out, if possible, on a level spot of ground. Lay one of the long edges of the compass base plate along the magnetic meridian on the map as shown, with the direction-of-travel arrow on the plate pointing to magnetic north. Turn the compass housing to 0°. With the compass and map "frozen" together, carefully turn the map until the north-pointing end of the needle lies directly over the compass-orienting arrow below. The map is now "oriented"; the map directions and land directions are one and the same.

With the map "glued" to the ground, pick up the compass and connect "here" to "there" as shown (Fig. 38). Always turn the housing until the north-pointing end of the needle lies over the orienting arrow (0°). Then you just stand behind the compass, read the "street number," and start for your first landmark. Although bee-line travel can be fun, it is not practical, at least in hilly or brushy country. Fig. 39 shows your usual problem and how to solve it.

Using the map in this way—always orienting it before taking a bearing or starting out on a course—you need give no thought to variation. If you want to draw magnetic meridians on the uncut map as shown by Kjellström, it's often not necessary to orient the map.[7] But I always like to do it anyway. Then I have a better feeling about where I'm going.

Beginners who follow these instructions do not get lost. Woodsmen with experience may get a "leetle mite careless." It's then that they may become confused for a spell when "there" doesn't show up where they thought it should be.

Besides the true-north and magnetic-north arrows on the map, the newer maps will show a grid north. Pay no attention to this unless you are interested in the Universal Thousand-Meter grid system shown by tick marks along the edges of the map. For information about this, ask the U.S.G.S. for their three-page mimeo MIO-80, "The UTM Grid on Geological Survey Maps."

If you really get interested in these maps, you'll want the collection of 25 ($18.75) chosen to illustrate the great variations in topography across this magnificent land of ours. Each day at camp, I posted on the bulletin board a new map with a few questions that could be answered from it. Next day, another map appeared beside the first one with answers to the previous day's questions, and a new list for the current map. At all times there were two maps on display, the old one and the new one. Once, when I pointed out a certain river and asked a camper in which direction it flowed, he glanced at it and said, "Northeast and southwest!" You and your campers can have a lot of fun with maps.

Orienteering

To quote from Kjellström's book: "With map and compass for your steady companions, the art of *Orienteering*—the skill of finding your way along highways and country roads, through woods and fields, through mountain territory and over lakes—becomes an intriguing hobby and an interesting sport, whether you travel alone or with a buddy or with a group of like-minded friends."[8] For many years in Sweden, this sport, which involves racing over a marked course, has had great success. And the idea has spread throughout the world.[9]

Fig. 38: White arrows show a 150° course line drawn on an oriented map, from road junction to lake. Turn this book around and sight along the travel arrow. This compass has a pace counter and magnifying lens.

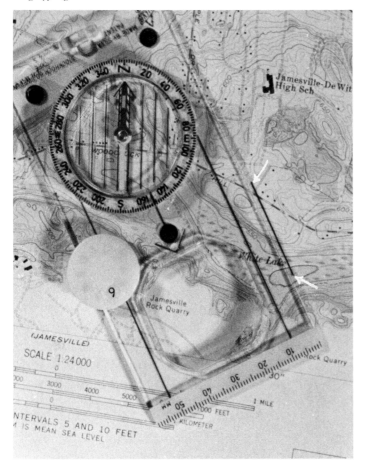

Fig. 39: (From Your Way with Map and Compass *by John Disley. Courtesy Silva Inc.)*

Commentary on the 3 routes:

A   Fast but very unsafe. It will be difficult to know exactly where to leave the highway. No attack point.

B   Very unsafe and tiring. A tough climb over the hill. Hard to stay on a compass course for such a long section.

C   Obviously the best choice. Quick and safe. The bend in the dirt road will make a fine attack point for the last few hundred feet/metres into control 2.

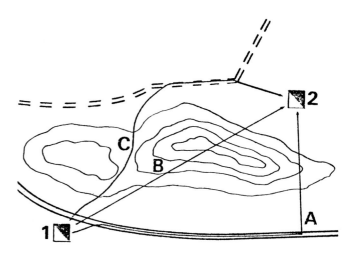

THE TOIL OF THE TRAIL

What have I gained by the toil of the trail?
I know and know well.
I have found once again the lore I had lost
In the loud city's hell.

I have broadened my hand to the cinch and the axe,
I have laid my flesh to the rain;
I was hunter and trailer and guide;
I have touched the most primitive wildness again.

I have threaded the wild with the stealth of the deer.
No eagle is freer than I;
No mountain can thwart me, no torrent appall,
I defy the stern sky.
So long as I live, these joys will remain,
I have touched the most primitive wildness again.

Hamlin Garland (1860-1940)

(Used by permission of his daughters, Constance Garland Doyle and Isabel Garland Lord.)

FROM HERE TO THERE

1. Page 80—U.S. Geological Survey, 1200 S. Eads St., Arlington, VA 22202.

2. Page 82—For an excellent evaluation of 10 models of the Silva compass and some 20 other makes, see Backpacker Magazine No. 13, February 1976.

3. Page 83—How to chart your course is described in great detail in Björn Kjellström's excellent *Be Expert with Map and Compass*. New York: Charles Scribner's Sons, 1967.

4. Page 84—Horace Kephart, *Camping and Woodcraft*. Riverside, NJ: Macmillan, 1972.

5. Page 84—Björn Kjellström, *Be Expert with Map and Compass*.

6. Page 86—The U.S. Geological Survey is the best source of maps for the hiker and camper. See above for eastern maps; for maps of areas west of the Mississippi, write the Survey in Denver, CO 80225. In Canada, write the Department of Mines and Technical Surveys, Ottawa. Ask the U.S.G.S. to send you an Index Map showing named quadrangles that cover the state or states where you wish to travel. Quadrangle maps cost $1.25 each. Ask also for the booklet, "Topographic Maps." It contains the map symbols that the Survey uses; you need them to interpret its maps. Local sporting-goods stores and some bookstores often have U.S.G.S. maps. Other maps may be obtained from the U.S. Forest Service, National Park Service, and state and local forestry or park departments.

7. Page 88—Björn Kjellström, *Be Expert With Map and Compass*.

8. Page 89—Björn Kjellström, *Be Expert With Map and Compass*.

9. Page 89—In the United States, you can write to the U.S. Orienteering Federation, Suite 317, 933 N. Kenmore St., Arlington, VA 22201 for information on competitive orienteering. The National Hiking and Ski Touring Association has a magazine, Better Camping, P.O. Box 7421, Colorado Springs, CO 80918, which has orienteering information.

WOODS WALKING AND TRAILCRAFT

One day the old woodsman was leading a group of Physical Education seniors along an Adirondack trail, when the one just behind him stepped on his heel. The reaction was immediate. The O.W. went into high gear, walking as fast as he could, and he never stopped or looked back until he came to a brook-crossing about a quarter of a mile from camp. Only a couple of the boys were still with him, and they, panting heavily, dropped to the ground. The rest were strung out along the trail, and it took them some time to catch up.

"Where's the fire?" said one.

"No fire," said the O.W., "but when someone steps on my heels, I'm going to get them out of the way!"

It has been shown many times that college athletes traveling through dense, trailless woods, can be brought to a point of exhaustion by an experienced woodsman twice or even three times their age. How can this be so? Stewart Edward White, woodsman and writer, in his 1903 book *The Forest*, gave three reasons why woods walking is so different from walking or running on a smooth surface. 1) No two successive steps are of the same length. 2) No two steps fall on the same quality of footing. 3) No two steps are on the same level.[1] The brush— young trees and shrubs—is sometimes so dense that it seems impossible to get through it. Often hidden in the brush are fallen tree trunks and old stumps barring your passage.

The experienced woodsman never tries to fight the brush. This is why I don't like the term "bushwhacking" to denote travel through trailless woods. Webster's definition, "to clear a path through thick woods especially by chopping down bushes and low branches," carries the wrong idea about good woods walking. And the word also means to attack from ambush! We need another word to describe our passage, leaving no mark of our having gone that way. Why not simply "bushwalk," used by Pamela Bell, an Australian, in Adirondack Life Magazine (March-April 1977)?

The woodsman can travel all day by going slowly and slipping through the brush. The trained athlete may look ahead and think, "Oh, this is easy. I can just force my way through." And he tries to do so, and goes too fast. If he is not exhausted by the end of the first hour, he will be soon thereafter. There is nothing more maddening, or damaging to the ego, than to find that you are indeed actually "bushed"!

So how do you learn to walk pleasurably in the woods? Certain techniques will in time become almost instinctive. When you walk, do you toe out appreciably? If so, you may not be using your feet to the best advantage. Man is the only one of earth's creatures with a typical heel-and-toe stride. The heel strikes first, the arch springs forward, and the big toe completes the movement. When you toe out, you throw out of balance the whole marvelous structure that is your foot. Toeing out also reduces the length of each step, and the loss counts up, at the end of the day, in distance covered.

However, proper foot position is only the beginning. You need to lift your feet higher when walking through the forest than you would on a well-trodden trail. If you don't, some protruding root, a hidden fallen branch, or a rock will trip you. You will also find that the heel-and-toe stride gets modified in the woods, so that you walk more nearly flat-footed. The knees may be slightly bent, and you develop a somewhat rolling gait, your whole walking machine on the alert to cushion and protect you from the frequent jolts given by the roughly uneven ground.

These few suggestions come from having walked through several kinds of forest over a span of 60 years. You may need a couple of seasons of woods travel before your feet get "educated." Then when you start out through the forest, those elastic feet, which never evolved to walk hard city pavements, suddenly come to life. They feel the rough places, lift you over fallen logs, stride across narrow gulches, hug the side of a steep ravine, or explore the possibility of safe footing over slippery rocks in the middle of a stream. Dr. Alexis Carrell, the famous physician, pointed out that our feet are most efficient and feel the best when walking over uneven ground. The irregularities help to support the arches. Most of our foot troubles come from improper shoes and from pounding hard pavements.

When climbing long or steep grades, the knees especially take a beating. You can rest them with the "limp step" method. After shifting your weight to the uphill leg with knee locked, let the downhill one go limp for a second or less before swinging it forward. Whenever you feel undue strain on the knees, do this several times with each leg.

The most important thing about all walking is the balance among breathing rate, heartbeat, and walking speed. Establish a rate of breathing that is comfortable, and try to keep it more or less constant. *Speed* is the variable. Before you start to pant, slow down! Paul Petzoldt, director of the National Outdoor Leadership School, calls this common-sense technique "Rhythmic Breathing."[2] It is the basis of his method for teaching foot traveling in the wilderness. R-B results in a steady energy output, minimizes body overheating, and lets you arrive at your destination less tired than if you had used the "run-and-stop" method too often followed by beginners.[3]

He who chooses to go on a bee-line through heavy brush when a trail is available is not wise in the ways of woodsmen. As Old Nessmuk once said, "We do not go to the green woods and crystal waters to rough it, we go to smooth it. We get it rough enough at home, in towns and cities."[4] So by all means use a trail if there is one. Two or three miles on a good trail may take less energy and time than a mile through dense forest. And a pointer or two here: You may be tempted to sail along the trail with your eyes far ahead, paying no attention to what's underfoot. If you do, you may find yourself flat on your face. There may be projecting roots, small round stones, and smooth, barkless, short sections of branches as large as your thumb. You might as well step up on a roller skate as upon one of these trail demons.

To save energy, especially when backpacking, never step onto any obstruction that you can step over, and never step over anything you can easily walk around. Did you ever wonder why a forest trail suddenly makes a detour to one side, returning soon to its previous course? You may still see the remains of a fallen tree where the trail circles. It was easier to walk around the tangle of branches than through it. As to stepping over a log, a friend from the South once said, "Oh no, you don't, at least not before you look on the other side —snake maybe."

So, in this vast land of ours, there are many kinds of forests and topography, each with its own local problems. In many of the open ponderosa-pine forests of the West, there is easy going, little brush, and a smooth springy carpet of pine needles to walk on. By contrast, some Florida jungles are almost impassable, and along the southern Appalachians are "rhododendron hells." One old-timer thought he'd shortcut through one, but the going got worse, and finally he could neither crawl under the dense growth nor force his way through. When he finally got out, someone asked how he did it.

"I swum over the tops," he said.

A common barrier is a stream. If it has a firm bottom and is not too cold, deep, wide, or fast-running, it may be best simply to wade it. Take off your boots and socks, and then put the boots on again. Lace them, wade across, take them off, pour out the water, wipe your feet dry, and put on socks and boots. If this seems too much of a nuisance, just wade across and then remove your boots and socks and squeeze water from the socks. Of course, if the stream is clear and the bottom is firm sand, you can keep both boots and socks dry by wading barefoot; but if it is rocky or muddy, keep your boots on. If the water is cloudy, explore the bottom ahead with a pole. If you have a belt strap on your pack, release it! More than one explorer has been drowned when he fell and couldn't free himself from his pack.

Perhaps you will have to cross on a tree trunk. Be very cautious. A bare trunk may be safer than one that is bark-covered—you can better judge the condition of the bare wood, and a bark-covered trunk may hide decay. Never cross on a birch log or trunk. The paper bark is unbelievably durable, but the wood inside soon decays and may be nothing but punk. You may walk halfway across before the log collapses, dropping you into the water. If you decide to use a log, cut or pick up a steadying pole for one hand and carry your pack in the other. Or sling the pack by one strap over a shoulder and use both hands on the pole. It may also be much safer not to walk across but rather to straddle the trunk and hitch or "coon" your way to the other side.

If you are going on a day's walk along well-marked, beaten trails, there may be few problems to mar the wonderful experience of a day in the woods. By all means learn to recognize the trees and other plants along the way. They can be your friends, and can tell you many interesting and important things. At your first rest stop, take time to look around and see how plants compete for space and for overhead light. Nowhere is the phrase "adapt or die" more fitting than in a forest. Look over there: see how an old tree trunk fell and hit a young tree and flattened it to the ground. Did the little tree give up? No. Now, after perhaps 10 years, it has developed a graceful curve and straightened itself.

How about timing that rest stop and the others to follow? Some will say to take a five-minute break every half-hour or a 10-minute one every hour. They must be thinking of open level ground. I agree with Robert S. Wood, who says in his book *Pleasure Packing,* "There is a myth that one should find a comfortable pace and then stick to it. Nothing could be further from the truth. The most common error among hikers is trying doggedly to maintain a set pace despite changes in grade."[5] To which I would add another deterrent to a steady pace: varying conditions of the terrain over which you're walking (rocky, muddy, deep dry sand, etc.).

The important thing is to stop *before* you use up your reserve energy. Give your body a few minutes to drain off accumulated fatigue acids. If there are several people in the group, you will have to set a pace that does not exhaust the one least able physically. And always remember that an extra stop is in order when something especially interesting appears: a grand view, a rare pileated woodpecker's square excavation on a tree trunk, or even a lowly ant staggering along under a load heavier than she is.

When you set out along a trail, what is your purpose? Must you reach a certain goal so that you can say later, in that faintly superior tone, "Oh, I've been there"? Or is the journey itself, with its myriad of impacts along the way, what's really important? In 60 years of woods travel, the infinite variety of nature has been such that I always see or otherwise experience something new on every trip. The great biologist and inspired teacher Louis Agassiz said, "I spent the summer traveling. I got halfway across my backyard." Somewhere between this approach and that of the hiker who wants only to reach his goal and looks neither to the right nor the left, there is desirable middle ground. Find it.

When you look at a trail on a map, you can only guess what it will be like. Of course, the much-advertised and heavily traveled trails may be veritable highways—but this is not a sure thing. Thousands of feet may have tramped the wetter parts into a quagmire a foot deep! Well, this is part of the adventure; but try to find little-used trails. They're more fun, and are a much greater challenge to you as a pathfinder. Trails often fork. Does this show on the map? Maybe not. Was this trail once an old logging road (look for ruts)? If so, then the angle between the two branches may be small, indicating a passing zone on a single-track road. The branches may come back together within a short distance to form one trail. This "ain't necessarily so"—one branch may slowly veer away and end up on the other side of nowhere, or gradually peter out and disappear entirely. Watch out for side trails that may be confusing on the way back. At such forks you may want to push a couple of sticks into the ground to mark the return trail.

Always be observant; every few minutes turn around and look back. You may be shocked that things look so different in the other direction. There always seems to be not one trail but two: one going out and the other coming back. Here is where the trained woodsman, with his knowledge of trees, has an advantage. On the way out he'll have noticed a towering gray-barked beech tree with two small spruces near it, or a fallen yellow birch trunk or many other things that are never even noticed by the city dweller. You see the things you've been trained to see. After I'd spent some 20 years teaching dendrology, it was rare for me not to register any tree within sight. But then one day I went woods prowling with an entomologist classmate. He kept pointing out tiny insect eggs, little caterpillars, obscure moths, wood-borer holes, and other insect signs that completely escaped me. I might as well have been blind! I presume a geologist would have missed both trees and bugs in his search for rocks.

You will rarely see any of the birds or other shy animals of the forest if you and your trail companions make a big racket. Loud voices, shrill whistling, and yelling have no place there. This is especially true now, when hordes of hikers seek to explore the mysteries of the silent wilderness. In many places they are destroying the very things they came to find.

Does it seem possible that some people, having attained a mountain summit, would amuse themselves by throwing stones or rolling small boulders down the slope? Well, they do. I'm sure you have your own feelings on the danger of such behavior. Quite often the trail may zigzag across very steep slopes. Never cut across these switchbacks. Descending, it's dangerous; and going either way, you promote erosion and trail damage. A cardinal rule for smokers: never smoke while hiking; it's too easy to forget and drop a lighted butt. If you must smoke, do it only when you stop to rest. When finished, be sure the last spark is out. Then "field strip" the cigarette. Tear the paper and sprinkle out the unburned tobacco. Roll up the paper into a little ball, push it into the ground, and cover it. Perhaps with the "new ethic," you'd better put it in your pocket and carry it out!

A given distance along a trail or through the woods is better measured by the time it takes to walk it than by the actual measurement in miles. This is because of the twists and turns, the ups and downs, the footing and obstructions along the way. Bob Marshall, when a student at Forestry Camp, used to ask experienced Adirondack guides the distances to nearby ponds or hilltops. The usual answer was, "Oh, about a mile and a half." Bob then timed the routes and found that the Adirondacker's mile and a half might be anything from two to four miles.

Unless you have to meet someone at a certain time, you might consider not carrying a watch. It's a new experience for most time-bound city dwellers. Can you relax and adapt to the daily rhythm of nature? It is something to try. At least one famous hiker says that he sometimes goes exploring without a map for more adventure. Most people find they get enough adventure even when they have a map; but for an experienced outdoorsman, it does indeed offer an additional challenge.

What does the ancient Sphinx have to do with exploring the outdoors on foot? Most people know only that the Sphinx is an enormous statue near Giza, Egypt. It is a winged lion's body with the head of a Pharoah that dates back to 2550 B.C. In an ancient Greek legend the Sphinx had a woman's head. The great beast dwelt on a mountaintop with her famous riddle, which no one could answer: "What has four feet, two feet, and three feet?" The trembling victim unable to answer was promptly gobbled up! Finally, Oedipus answered the challenge: "Man, who first crawls on all fours, then stands on two legs, and as evening approaches walks with a staff." Whereupon with a great cry the Sphinx threw herself down from the mountain.

Perhaps my father prejudiced me with this fable told some 65 years ago, but I've never yet had to use cane or staff, for which I'm very grateful. Having said this, I add quickly that a walking stick or staff has some very useful features, especially in open country. ("Thy rod and thy staff, they comfort me.") But most of my experience has been in the dense forests of the eastern U.S., and I've never seen even one old Adirondack guide (unless crippled) using a cane or staff. When I'm bushwalking cross-country, I want *both* hands free. Along good trails or in the open, a walking stick can be most comforting. I suspect it's a throwback to early times when a stout stick was a weapon, later replaced by the spear and sword. Colin Fletcher writes delightfully about his 4½-foot bamboo staff, companion of many years on the trail. He lists not only its many uses but also its disadvantages.[6]

I might not even have mentioned this "third leg" except that hollow light metal ones with storage space inside are not being advertised in the catalogs —and it gave me the chance to tell the classical fable of the Sphinx! Also, you'll find an excellent story by Bill Woodraska on his "Survival Staff" in Wilderness Camping Magazine, July-August 1972. Starting with a 4½-foot, 1¼-inch-diameter aluminum tube, he packages no less than 22 survival items which slip neatly inside. Tube weight is one pound; items, two pounds, which lightens the pack by that much. However, it still takes energy to swing it.

WOODS WALKING AND TRAIL CRAFT

1. Page 91—Stewart Edward White, *The Forest*. The Outlook Co., 1903. You need the library for this one: it's long out of print.
2. Page 92—Paul Petzoldt, *The Wilderness Handbook*. New York: W.W. Norton, 1974.
3. Page 92—For more on walking, see Horace Kephart, *Camping and Woodcraft*. Riverside, NJ: Macmillan, 1972.
4. Page 92—Nessmuk (G.W. Sears), *Woodcraft*. New York: Dover Publications, 1963.
5. Page 93—Robert S. Wood, *Pleasure Packing*. Berkeley, CA: Condor Books, 1972.
6. Page 94—Colin Fletcher, *The New Complete Walker*. New York: Alfred A. Knopf, 1974.

nerable parts of your body for losing heat. All this would be bad enough; but now the wind, which blew lazily and warm from the south before the storm, has switched around to the northwest and is blowing an icy gale.

BEWARE HYPOTHERMIA

WIND-CHILL CHART

actual thermometer reading (°F.)

Estimated wind speed in MPH	50	40	30	20	10	0
Equivalent temperature (°F)						
Calm	50	40	30	20	10	0
5	48	37	27	16	6	−5
10	40	28	16	4	−9	−21
15	36	22	9	−5	−18	−36
20	32	18	4	−10	−25	−39
25	30	16	0	−15	−29	−44
30	28	13	−2	−18	−33	−48

(This well-known table shows that with a temperature of 40°F. and a wind speed of 20 m.p.h. the equivalent temperature is only 18°F. above zero! But remember that these figures are based on the exposure of bare, dry skin. On skin protected by one or more layers of dry clothing and a wind breaker, the wind-chill effect is very much less. But wet cotton clothing gives practically no protection.)

Hypothermia, the progressive cooling of the body's "core" below its normal temperature, is the No. 1 killer of outdoors people. You might think that this danger exists only in winter. Not so—most cases of hypothermia occur at temperatures of 30° to 50°F. How does it happen? In our so-called "temperate" climate, a sudden summer rainstorm may drop the temperature 30° within a few minutes. Before the storm, it was a pleasant sunshiny 70°, and you were hiking, or fishing, or paddling a canoe. Now it is only 40°, and your cotton bluejeans or shorts and cotton shirt are soaking wet. This in itself might be lethal, due to the cooling effect of evaporation (except at 100 percent relative humidity). Further, like millions of others you are hatless, and during the storm, 50° rain pelted your bare head and neck, the most vul-

That cold blast of wind is cooling your body much faster than you may think. You begin to shiver. But maybe you are near the top of a mountain and just have to get there. Although still soaking wet, you climb faster, and perhaps the added energy output makes you feel warmer. But now without sensing it, you are making the final lethal error—pushing yourself to exhaustion. Your body is losing energy through heat, faster than it's being produced—your temperature is still sliding downward.

Without knowing it, you are beginning to die. To survive, you *must at once* get out of the wind, take shelter, build a fire, strip off your wet clothes, and put on dry wool ones. Eat some high-energy food—chocolate bars or other candy, or, best of all, honey. *Hypothermia is the killer of the unprepared or ignorant.* People who stay warm and dry, nibble frequently, and do not drive themselves to exhaustion do not get hypothermia.

If you are a group leader during cold, wet, windy weather, THINK HYPOTHERMIA and watch yourself and your companions for these symptoms:

1) Uncontrollable fits of shivering.
2) Vague, slow, slurred speech.
3) Memory lapses. Incoherence.
4) Immobile or fumbling hands.
5) Frequent stumbling. Lurching gait.
6) Drowsiness (to sleep is to die).
7) Apparent exhaustion. Inability to get up after a rest.

Don't believe what the patient says about how he feels—his brain is numb. Believe the symptoms! Besides the above-mentioned steps, give warm drinks—preferably sweetened with honey. Few people know that the sucrose in flower nectar is split in the honeybee's stomach to form two simple sugars which, upon being swallowed, quickly enter the human bloodstream.

Get your patient naked and into a warm sleeping bag. Of course, the bag itself gives no heat. It only conserves that given off by what's inside it. If feasible, place well-wrapped warm rocks or canteens of warm water alongside the person. Best of all, especially if the patient is in the last stages (semiconscious, etc.), try to keep him awake, and have a naked "heat donor" slip into the bag with him. If you can rig a double bag, use two donors—one on each side. Skin-to-skin contact is the best treatment.

Death from "exposure" has been recognized for ages, but apparently hypothermia is still a new word and an unfamiliar diagnosis to many people. Recently, a young girl got "chilled" on a raw autumn day at a picnic. She had fits of shivering and became incoherent. She was rushed to the emergency room of a big city hospital. The standard checkup showed nothing more than a lowering of normal body temperature by a couple of degrees. Meantime she was slowly warming up; several hours later she was discharged. The interns were mystified!

GOING
IT
ALONE

Relatively speaking, there are but a few who ever hear and answer the siren call of Far Places. This is fortunate for the large numbers of land managers and rescue teams who run risks, sweat, and spend much money each year searching for individual hikers who get lost or don't arrive at their check-in point within a reasonable time as planned. If it could be enforced, I'd favor collecting a nominal insurance fee from lone hikers—not to discourage them but to help cover costs of search and rescue.

More than one hiking club advises most emphatically that the minimum number in a travelling group should be four. Then if one is injured and cannot walk, there are three others to divide the necessary care, including, perhaps, going for help. Millions of hikers have never heard or pay no attention to this safety rule. Actually, the chances of incapacitating injuries "out there" are far less than the constant danger in city traffic which we casually accept.

Rudyard Kipling, in his magnificent poem "The Explorer," wrote: "Til a voice, as bad as Conscience, rang interminable changes/On one everlasting Whisper day and night repeated—so:/Something hidden. Go and find it. Go and look behind the ranges—/Something lost behind the Ranges. Lost and waiting for you. Go!"[1] Many of us pierced in youth by these compelling words were launched on a quest that had far greater meaning than merely going alone through some woods or over some mountains.

Long before recorded history, young boys on the threshold of manhood would detach themselves from the protective family or tribe and go off into the forest or desert to "dream dreams, and see visions"—in modern terms, to "find themselves." Fasting might be part of the ritual. In many tribes, the seeker acquired a lifetime secret name that symbolized his identity and was known only to himself. Mother Earth, Father Sky, and the Great Spirit still challenge their more sophisticated sons and daughters to some such experience. Once having had the experience, they are apt to renew it at intervals throughout the rest of their lives. This is the Great Reason we must keep as much remaining wild land as possible—even remnants.

There are some other reasons, of course—"practical" ones, such as the use by many hunters and fishermen who are not only impelled by the ancestral love of the chase but also, deep down, crave temporary solitude. To experience solitude, Steve Van Matre in his book *Acclimatizing* has developed some excellent techniques for camp groups and other outdoors people. Under the heading "Walden Solo," he writes: "With the solitude comes a special kind of freedom—to think, to feel, and to be as one wishes. In his own place, half of a mile square in area, the young person can explore and contemplate and absorb the workings of nature."[2]

Solitude implies Silence—at least part of the time. How many moderns have ever experienced *absolute silence*? Most people these days seem terrified by it. From the time the alarm clock jars them awake until at day's end they drift off to sleep soothed by radio music, they are encompassed by sound. We humans are ambivalent about *sound-silence*. After being buffeted by sound long enough, we may crave "silence"—but not for long! Complete silence may bring "peace to your soul," or it can bring complete terror.

Many writers have tried to make this clear. Robert W. Service writes: "...the icy mountains hemmed you in with a Silence you most could *hear* ...and the Silence that bludgeons you dumb...." But later, we find: "...it's the beauty that thrills me with wonder, it's the stillness that fills me with peace."[3] In the early 1870s, Verplanck Colvin conducted the first extensive *Topographical Survey of the Adirondack Wilderness.*[4] He often met and was offered the services of inexperienced young men romantically attracted to the Big Woods. Knowing that most of them would be useless there, he included in his 1873 Report a statement on the working conditions of a typical young surveyor in the wilderness at a barometer station, making readings every five minutes dawn to dark, "day after day alone at his station, companionless, and inclosed by the deep awful silence of the wilderness..." And Nessmuk wrote: "Silence broods over the cold still forest."[5]

My own first confrontation with wilderness silence was unusually strange. Robert Marshall, a student at our college, was a sophomore when I was a freshman. We met for the first time playing scrub lacrosse and were friends thereafter. While at the college's summer camp on Cranberry Lake in the western Adirondacks, Bob decided to spend his weekends exploring the surrounding country, especially to visit the many ponds that dotted the map. By the end of the summer he had seen 94 of them, travelling through much trailless wilderness to do so. He then wrote a narrative, and in his typical methodical way included several lists—one of them rating each pond according to its relative beauty from 1 to 94. He liked doing things like that, and enjoyed the arguments that such lists provoked. That autumn, he loaned me his "Weekend Trips in the Cranberry Lake Region," and after reading it, I was hooked.

So it was that the next June, late one afternoon, I was following a dim trail around the bends of the slow-moving, silent Oswegatchie River. The Cranberry Lake map was marked "beaver dam" at only one place on the entire quadrangle. There were many beaver dams in the area, so I thought this one on the Oswegatchie must be an unusually big one. The sun was going down, casting long shadows of the towering white pines along the trail. It was time to camp—the dam could wait until the next day.

Rounding the bend in the river, I came upon a knoll, and clambered to its low, flat top—a perfect place to camp. When I slipped off my pack, the sudden release of its 35 pounds made every step feel as though I had winged feet!

I looked around. The heavy layer of needles had to be removed to create a safe fire spot. I noticed a depression in the smooth surface, and began scooping away the needles. About three or four inches down, I suddenly contacted charcoal. A long time ago, some camper, hunter, or fisherman had used this very place. I would be kindling my fire on the bare sand just below where his charcoal layer had been. And now, for the first time, I began to feel the Absolute Silence. It was eerie. It seemed to press heavily on my ears. I could indeed almost hear it. It was that time of the diurnal cycle when the day creatures prepare for sleep and the night prowlers are barely awake. A profound hush prevailed.

A small campfire, a steaming kettle of rice and raisins, and soon after to bed. How long I slept I do not know. I dreamed that a tall, evil-faced one stood over me, hand raised to strike. I woke up. It was cloudy, and pitch black under the pines—and that awesome Silence. Sight and hearing did not exist.

Then it happened. The canopy of silence was torn into a million shreds by a "cannon shot" from the invisible river just below. Had I known what it was, I would have been startled enough, but I did not know until several weeks later, in daylight, in a pond many miles away. But for now, again the Great Silence. At that moment, a steam-railroad engineer on an unheard train some seven miles to the east sounded the traditional crossing signal ("Q" in Morse Code). I heard it as a faint *wooo-wooo-woo-wooo*. I wish he could have known what he did for a scared youngster spending his first night alone in the depths of the Adirondack wilderness. He brought me back to reality. I went to sleep and the next morning continued upstream to the beaver dam, still not knowing that one of the furry clan had shattered the silence by slapping the water with his broad flat tail. I never had such an experience again, and soon became accustomed to the solitude of the wilderness. But, especially if you are city born and bred, there is not only physical but also psychological adventure "out there."

GOING IT ALONE

1. Page 98—Rudyard Kipling, "The Explorer." *A Kipling Anthology*. London: Methuen & Co. Ltd., 1922. 201 pp. Be sure to read the entire poem. You'll never forget it. I memorized it 50 years ago, and it is forever a part of my being.

2. Page 98—Steve Van Matre, *Acclimatizing: A Personal and Reflective Approach to a Natural Relationship*. Martinsville, IN: American Camping Association, 1974, page 208.

3. Page 99—Robert W. Service, *The Spell of the Yukon*. New York: Barse and Hopkins, 1907.

4. Page 99—Verplanck Colvin, *Topographical Survey of the Adirondack Wilderness*. 1873. This is a rare reference book.

5. Page 99—Nessmuk (G.W. Sears), *Woodcraft*. New York: Dover, 1963.

LOST!

The very word often strikes terror to the soul. It calls to mind stories you've read in books, magazines, and newspapers of someone who gets separated from a group and wanders aimlessly through the forest for days. Such people—unprepared for this experience—soon exhaust themselves. They panic and do all kinds of illogical things, such as crossing a good trail to plunge again, unseeing, back into the brush on the other side. When far gone, a lost person may even try to run away from his rescuers!

All of the advice that can be given for getting out alive and in good condition rests upon one premise—that you *don't panic!* If you do, you may indeed be a gone goose—it's that serious.

Those of us who've loved and explored the wild places since childhood find it difficult to understand how strangers to the woods may feel—even when not lost. Recently, several inner-city teenagers were taken for the first time some 15 miles out into the countryside. They arrived at a day camp on the edge of the woods. It was early in the season, and only the resident director was there. He met them and suggested a hike. They looked around and spotted his trailer. One of them said, "You live out here all alone?"

"Sure," he said, "why not?"

"Aren't you scared?"

"Of course not. Why should I be?" And so they strung out behind him along the trail, which soon entered the forest. After a short distance, he happened to glance over his shoulder and saw something astonishing. Instead of being spaced single-file, they were right on his heels and bunched together as close to each other as possible! Nobody needed to tell the director how these supposedly "hardbitten" city kids felt about this strange environment. He stopped right there and called up all his outdoor-leadership talents to make them feel more at ease.

To change the scene for a moment, consider the AmerIndian lad separated from his companions on a hunt. He's not seen any of them for several hours. The sun is low in the west. He suddenly realizes that he's gone beyond the usual hunting ground. The forest is no longer familiar, but he feels none of the fear that might overcome a city boy lost for the first time. Why? Because all of this is his home. From earliest childhood he's been taught as part of his religion that the earth is his mother, the sky his father, and over all is the Great Spirit. Can those born and raised in cities ever learn to feel this way? They should try.

Kephart quotes an old woodsman: "There's no use in offering advice to novices about what they should do if they get lost, because a lost man is an insane man, anyway, and will remember nothing that has been told him."[1] Kephart says that the first time he was lost he was "rattled and shook all over." He had an overpowering urge to start running headlong toward where he felt camp was. But he did remember that this would be the worst thing he could do. He did what you must do. Stop, sit down for about half an hour, and try to give fear a chance to drain away. Force yourself to look down at the little world underfoot: there is a tiny ant dragging an enormous load over almost impossible obstacles. A blue jay

101

flying through the woods sees you and veers away as he gives his raucous call. Glance up a tree trunk to the sky overhead. All this was home for our distant ancestors. Why should you fear it? As Thoreau said, "Nothing is so much to be feared as fear." Until you can banish enough of it so you can think straight, you might just as well stay right where you are. In many situations this is the best thing to do anyway.

Having recovered your senses, start saying, "I must *conserve my energy.*" This is the most important of all. If you were part of a group and strayed away from the trail, perhaps to follow a bird, you probably hurried in trying to get back and are all tuckered out. From now on every thing you do must be unhurried and well thought out. If you were part of a group, by now you'll have been missed and a search will have started—that is, unless the sun is about to set. So while you're just "setting," overcoming your fright, every five minutes give a loud holler. You may be heard. Also, listen—not only for signals from your party but also for traffic sounds, especially from trucks laboring up a long grade. A road may be nearer than you think it could be.

If it's morning or early afternoon, you still have some time to run out a few leisurely traverses, hoping to pick up the trail or a travelled road. But before you leave, mark your "headquarters." Find three long poles and tie them together tipi fashion. Everyone should carry a pencil and 3 × 5-inch scratch pad. Leave a note up high on the tripod, giving your name, the date, what you are about to do, and the time.

The following suggestions assume that you don't have compass or map. If you do, and know how to use them, most of this chapter should be superfluous; but on day hikes with a group, only the leader may have these things. As you move slowly away from your tripod or other marker, keep glancing back. Before it gets difficult to see, reach overhead and snap a small tree branch so that it hangs down. Keep marking your way with these "flags." Be sure to make a new one before losing sight of the last one. With these markers you can find your way back to your base.

You should now consider that you may have to stay out in the woods all night. You'll need *water, fire, windbreak,* and *bed.* You're lucky if you have a few hours of daylight left to look for these things or their makings. It's assumed, of course, that you do have matches and a sharp knife. If it's almost sunset, you may have to depend upon what's at hand. Drag

in sound, dry wood, or break off dead branches from nearby trees—about four times as much as you guess you'll need. Kephart suggested that you rake away the leaves, and on the bare strip build a narrow, body-length fire. This will dry out and warm the soil. Later you can remove the coals and ashes and lay boughs there for a bed. In a broadleaf forest, where the thin layer of leaves is easily removed, this may be safe. In a coniferous forest, which has a thick humus layer, it would be highly dangerous. And it would take a lot of energy, which you don't have. If you can find a large fallen log to use as a reflector, pile some leaves or evergreen boughs along it for a bed, and build a safe fire out front.

But even all this isn't absolutely necessary. Enos Mills, mountaineer and great nature guide, spent many a night just sitting and leaning against a tree trunk with a bright, warm little fire out front. He would doze off for a while and then, when the fire died down and the cold woke him up, he'd add more wood to the fire and go back to sleep. This would be repeated several times during the night. He roamed the Colorado Rockies (especially Long's Peak) for over 20 years. He spoke of the "campfire's magic tent of light," and closed his book with: "A campfire in the forest is the most enchanting place on life's highway by which to have a lodging for the night."[2]

So now it's morning. What are your plans for the day? It may be just as well to build up the fire, add enough wet leaves or rotten wood to keep a good smoke rising—and wait. Two smoky fires 50 feet apart are better than one as a signal. Soon a helicopter or plane will probably spot your location, and a rescue party will be on the way. Assuming you have water and keep conserving your energy, the matter of food is not too important. People often go without food for many days and still survive. But you say you're hungry. Well, so are millions of others scattered around the world. The difference is that you may lack food for a day or two—or three. They will be on the edge of starvation all their lives. If you *definitely* know certain wild foods, help yourself, although quite often they don't seem to be available when needed most. Never experiment with unknowns. It's better to go hungry than to get poisoned.

What more can I say? Whether you wait to get found, or hike out to civilization, depends so much upon the season, the weather, how you are clothed, and the kind of country surrounding you that only general principles can be given. For many years, the advice was to follow streams, which would eventually lead to civilization. Although that's more or less true, there are many pitfalls and exceptions to this method. Nowadays, especially in mountainous or hilly regions, the advice is to climb, hoping to find a bare spot from which you can be seen from the air. Before starting out, do you see an easily climbable tree nearby? From its top you may be able to see the solution to your problem and know which way to head. But you may find that seemingly endless woods extend to the horizon—no mountains or prominent hills anywhere. If you were *not* with a group, did you obey the ironclad rule of letting someone know the general area where you were going and about when you might return and check in? If you did, just stay put and keep tending those two smoky fires. You'll be found. If you were foolhardy enough to just vanish into the wilderness, leaving no word, it may take longer.

There are few places in the populous eastern U.S. where you can go in a straight line for 10 miles or so without finding some sign of man—power lines, roads. Again, if you do leave your base camp, be sure to mark your trail so rescuers can follow you. For a couple of hours at a time you can use the moving sun or tree shadows on the ground to keep you from circling; or line up trees ahead of you.

The word "panic" is from Pan, the ancient Greek god of forests, pastures, and flocks. He had the head, chest, and arms of a man, the legs of a goat, and perhaps also a goat's ears and horns. Although Pan was the patron of shepherds, hunters, and fishermen, he could cause sudden unreasoning fear in humans. So when you panic in the wild, Pan is there—laughing at you. When you're lost, go slowly, keep Pan off your back, and all should be well.

LOST!

1. Page 101—Horace Kephart, *Camping and Woodcraft*. Riverside, NJ; Macmillan, 1972.
2. Page 102—Enos A. Mills, *Wild Life on the Rockies*. Boston: Houghton Mifflin, 1922.

USEFUL WILD PLANTS
Cattail, Basswood, Paper Birch

A subject as important and comprehensive as this one can only be touched upon here. There are several good books on edible and otherwise useful plants listed in the references. Learning about them can be a lifelong adventure.

The Cattail

Widely distributed over the face of the earth, one or another species of this plant forms dense pure stands on low-lying flats that are wet during most of the year (Fig. 40). To explore a flooded cattail marsh in late spring is an unforgettable experience. Rubber boots will keep the feet dry, but on a warm day, why worry about getting wet feet? Soaring aloft from the cattail's submerged stems and roots are the waving, flexible leaves, each one a

marvel of internal structure. I used to worry about the danger of breaking through the mat of stems and roots into the underlying muck, but the density of the mat is unbelievable, and in thick stands there seems to be little danger. However, in times of extra-high water (four to five feet), large sections of the buoyant mat may separate and float on the surface. In this case a would-be explorer should wait for a later date when the water has receded.

The brown, cylindrical cattail of late summer or autumn is familiar to almost everyone. Fastened with wire to a stout, green stick and dipped in kerosene, it can be used as a temporary torch. During winter and early spring, the millions of tightly compacted, cottony seeds loosen and are lofted by the wind. A single cattail may hold 500,000 of them. New cattails in spring are at first double affairs. The part at the top is an excellent vegetable while it is still green and covered by a leafy sheath. Remove the sheath, break off the top half, boil in salted water for about 15 minutes, and eat with butter like corn on the cob. They are tasty, having a somewhat nutty flavor.

Later in the year, the top half develops into mature, tightly packed stamens bursting with pollen. At the right time, you can collect this pollen by jarring the stem. Out it comes in a golden cloud. The pollen is high in protein and can be used as an extender when you make pancakes or biscuits. Three quarters flour and one quarter pollen are about right. When the pollen has been shed, the male flowers drop off, leaving a slender spike above the developing female cattail.

In spring, cut off some of the cattail-bearing stems at the base, and sever their basal ends into 12-to-18-inch pieces. Pull off the leaves. In the center of the remaining stem is the white pith known as "Cossack asparagus." Try cooking some. Russian officers have said that only in the Don Valley of their homeland are these any good, but you will find that our plants also are quite edible.

Below ground, the stout stems (*rhizomes*) are high in starch and are good survival food. They can be gnawed raw but taste much better when cooked, especially in spring when some of the starch changes to sugar. They are not easy to gather. If you just pull on the leaves, they will break off. A shovel or spade is usually needed to dig up the rhizomes. If hungry enough, you can probably pry some of them up with stout sticks. Peel off the outer "skin" and spongy layer; inside is the white core. The Indians dried it

Fig. 40: 1) Cattails in spring. Cattail from the previous year is on the left. On the right, a new double cattail—male at top, female below. 2) Hand-weaving a mat from cattail leaves. 3) Spoonful of pollen. 4) Exposed starchy stem and roots.

and with mortar and pestle made a fine flour.

As final gifts, cattail leaves can be woven into such things as mats and blankets. Dry the green leaves; moisten them just before use to remove brittleness. The autumn "fluff" from the seed spike can be used to stuff pillows or comforters.

Basswood

This tree got its name not from a fish but from the strong "bast" or bark fibers, which were well-known to the woodland Indians and used by them to make excellent hand-twisted string and rope. Basswood is a prolific sprouter as shown in Fig. 41. Assuming you have permission, these sprouts, perhaps two to six inches in diameter, can be cut. This should be done in spring or early summer while the tree is actively forming new wood and bark. At other times, bark peeling may be difficult if not impossible. The freshly peeled bark can be split into thongs that are very useful in camp.

To make good cordage requires more time. The quickest way to get strands soft enough to twist is to boil the bark in a water solution of wood ashes. This can be done on and off for several days when the campfire is burning. When the bark seems soft enough, wash it to remove the wood-ash lye solution you've made. Cordage made from such material is somewhat rough and not as pleasing as that made from bark soaked for one or two months. Make a bundle or coil of the freshly peeled bark, and weight it down with stones on the bottom of a pond or stream. You can take it out every two to three weeks to see whether it is soft enough to twist. The time needed will depend upon temperature and, probably, the population of microorganisms that "eat" the soft tissues and leave the bast fibers, which should easily separate into beautiful, raffia-like strips.

Look at Fig. 41 to see how cordage is twisted. Take a moist strip about three feet long and loop it over the little finger so that the ends are of unequal length, one perhaps a foot longer than the other. Now twist as shown. The strand away from you is twisted away and crossed toward you over the other one. As you hold the twist, pinch it with the left thumb and forefinger so that it won't untwist. Then let go with the right hand, reach over, twist the other strand, and keep repeating the process. You can soon release the little finger as the cord becomes longer. When you get within six inches of the short end, lay in another strand that will extend some distance beyond the long one and so keep going.

The Indians knew that their bark ropes were lighter, softer on the hands, and did not kink as readily as the white man's Manila cordage. They made their ropes 100 feet or so in length for hauling fish traps and for other purposes. One time I made a ⅝-inch, 10-foot, three-strand basswood rope and took it with me when I was visiting summer camps. Thrown over a tree limb, it supported my 155 pounds. I sometimes challenged any six youngsters, three on a side, to break it in a tug of war. If you want an emergency fish line, you can pick out enough fiber threads from the fresh bark with your knife. If they are too stiff to twist, chew them gently —not so hard that the fibers are broken.

Besides basswood, there are other trees—including the elms, mulberry, and cedars—that have fibrous bark. Some herbaceous plants can be used for fibers—especially milkweed stems. If you can find some last-year's milkweed stems lying on the ground, you will have fibers aplenty.

Basswood buds are edible raw or cooked, especially in spring. A botany professor once was scouting for blister-rust disease on white pine. He pulled his boat partway onto an island beach and went exploring inland. When he returned, his boat had blown offshore, and it was three days before his companions found him. All he had to eat were basswood buds and gulls' eggs. Afterward he said that at least the basswood buds were fresh! And dried basswood flowers make an excellent tea.

The wood of basswood is soft but tough, and is excellent for carving. The Iroquois Falseface Society made masks carved right on the tree. When finished, they were split off and then hollowed out.

Paper Birch

A more beautiful or useful tree would be hard to find. It has an enormous range across Canada from Newfoundland to Alaska, dipping into the northern United States and along the Appalachians. In thousands of summer camps, paper birch (white, or canoe birch) is a common tree, much admired chiefly for its dazzling bark, which makes it stand out from all other trees in the forest.

Birch bark was indispensable to the woodland Indians. A square sheet could be turned up at the corners and pinned to make a cooking pot. You can do this yourself—provided the flames do not get above the water level inside. Few things catch fire more easily than birch bark. Being waterproof, it

Fig. 41: Basswood. 1) Old tree and sprouts. 2) Iroquois false face. 3) Edible bud (enlarged). 4) Twisting bark cordage. 5) A three-strand bark rope.

never gets wet—even with surface water on it, it blazes immediately when touched with the flame from a match. Baskets, boxes, fish creels, dippers, picture frames, snow goggles, archery quivers, pails, notebook covers, writing paper, and lean-to roofing are only a few of the many things that can be made from white-birch bark. To the Indian, most important was the bark canoe, still made by them in the Canadian woods.

Bark utensils should be made with the inner surface outside, since it is tough and does not peel. Fig. 42 illustrates a waterproof birch-bark container sewed with the fine roots of spruce. If not used when dug, spruce roots can be stored dry and soaked to restore their flexibility. The rim of the vessel is reinforced with a barked, green, split-in-half twig from a willow or other kind of tree whose twigs can be bent without breaking.

Hard, dry nodules of wound pitch can be found on old spruce trees. Pry off some of these, and boil them in a bag made from coarse orange sacking. Some of the pitch may rise to the top and can be skimmed off. Most of it stays inside with bark fragments and other debris. Fish out the bag, place it on a flat stone, and roll out the pitch, using a short, two-inch-diameter branch section. The Indians liked their seams colored black, so they mixed some powdered charcoal in with the melted pitch. They applied hot pitch to canoes and utensils. The nodules pried from the tree are the chewing gum of the North Woods. You hold one in your mouth for a while to warm and soften it. Then you cautiously begin to chew. If the nodule is too dry it will break up into a bitter powder; if too soft it will stick to every tooth in your head; but if just right, you'll have a dandy chew. It can be saved and chewed several times before it gets powdery.

To get back to birch bark: *never peel it from a live tree.* That would be like slashing a work of art. When the papery bark is removed, the inner, green living bark is revealed. Unless this too is removed, the tree will not die—but it can never again grow papery bark where it was skinned. The wound blackens and becomes unsightly. For starting a fire, you can usually find naturally shed pieces on the ground, or perhaps a fallen dead tree. Paper birch tends to grow in clumps of two or more. Since it needs plenty of light, cutting one or more trunks may improve the growth of those remaining, and give you a great store of bark for making things.

When you've peeled the sheets from the tree in spring or early summer, roll them with the inside out and tie the roll. At camp, lay the sheets flat on the ground, and place rocks or small log sections on the pile to keep it from curling. Since birch bark never decays, ground storage is preferred to dry storage in a building, where the bark may get too brittle to work with easily. Tin shears are ideal for cutting the bark, but if a knife is used, the blade works easiest when held at a 45° angle. Of course, before a tree is felled, permission must be obtained.

After removing the white outer bark, take some pieces of the green inner bark, dry them, and pound them into a powder. The Indians used this as an emergency food. Cut up the trunk and branches. After thorough drying, birch makes excellent firewood.

A final gift from white birch is its sweet sap. Obtained in early spring by tapping the tree, it can be boiled down to syrup.[1]

USEFUL WILD PLANTS

1. Page 108—Be sure to get a copy of the Dover Publication reprint of Frances Densmore's *How Indians Use Wild Plants for Food, Medicine, and Crafts.* New York: 1974. It is full of ancient Chippewa lore and legends—including the story about how the white birch is the child of the Thunder Birds, and hence is never struck by lightning!

108

Fig. 42: Birchbark waterproof container, coil of spruce roots used in sewing the seams.

POISONOUS PLANTS

At once, poisonivy comes to mind. (It should be written as one word because it is not an ivy, such as English ivy.) The ancient rhyme:

Leaflets three, quickly flee (let it be)
Berries white, poisonous sight

is illustrated in Fig. 43. The complete leaf, with its three leaflets, is arranged with others in alternate order along the woody twig. Poisonivy commonly grows as a vine, creeping unobtrusively through the grass, spilling over old stone walls, or climbing fences and trees.

There are other plants with three leaflets. The box-elder tree, when young, often has this feature, but the leaves are opposite (paired) on the woody stem. Until you know the plants of your region well, however, it is best to avoid anything with "leaflets three." Some 60 kinds of birds eat poisonivy fruits containing the seeds, which are then dropped, especially where birds roost. In pine groves, poisonivy often almost covers the ground.

You cannot get the rash (*dermatitis*) by walking near the plant, or even by touching it. But the entire plant (root, stem, leaf) contains special internal poison canals, and if you break or bruise a leaf, the poison leaks out and sticks to your skin. Everyone at birth has a certain resistance to the poison, but it is foolhardy to test this out intentionally by bruising the leaves or otherwise getting the sticky juice on your body. After the first reaction, you may become sensitized for life and are then allergic to extremely small amounts of the poison.

Many cases of poisoning result from handling objects that have bruised the plant. The chief offenders are shoes. You go walking through the woods and fields, not knowing that you have stepped on poisonivy growing with other greenery. Then you handle your shoes and become contaminated. In most cases, the palms of the hands and soles of the feet are somewhat resistant. But a person might, not knowing that he or she has been poisoned, handle other, more sensitive parts of the body— often with dire results. A golfer did not know that his ball bounced once and bruised a poisonivy leaf in the rough before sailing back onto the green—he "got it." The family dog rolled in a patch of poisonivy and then crawled under the dining room table at lunch; the two barefooted children wriggled their toes in the dog's hair. A gardner digging with a trowel in a newly spaded lot unknowingly broke some poisonivy roots. He then touched the blade to which the juice adhered. Other important and common places of contamination are the door handles and steering wheel of your car.

In all these cases and many others, the contaminated article may retain the poison for a year or more after contact. You can wash the poison off nonporous articles with alcohol while wearing rubber gloves. With shoes and clothing (and pets) it's a different matter. Try repeated washing with strong soap suds. The best preventive is to recognize the plant and *keep away from it*. In autumn, its golden-to-red leaves are very attractive; people sometimes cut the woody stems and bring them indoors for decoration. Of course, the poison canals in the twig are thus severed and leak sticky fluid which contaminates the knife or clipper.

Fig. 43: Poisonivy. 1) Winter Twig. 2) Leaf. 3) Fruit. (From Textbook of Dendrology *(6th ed) by W.M. Harlow, E.S. Harrar, and F.M. White.)*

111

The poison penetrates the skin very rapidly —then there is little to do except to make the itching, burning, reddened skin more comfortable. If any large area or the eyes are affected, consult a dermatologist at once. There are other kinds of dermatitis so similar to that of poisonivy that only an expert can tell them apart. There are at least 250 remedies that have been used to relieve the burning itch. Calamine lotion has been used for many years as a standard remedy. Wet dressing of a Domeboro powder-water solution are also helpful. Your corner drugstore will have several other nonprescription formulations, but some of them may cause side effects in certain people. As your body fights the effect of the poison, blisters form. The fluid from these blisters is harmless and will not spread the allergy.

Two more observations. Never try to eradicate these plants by burning. The smoke carries bits of "tar" containing the poison. If the smoke touches you, you are probably in for a bad time. You may find poisonivy in the strangest places. I once found a luxuriant growth of it reaching some 20 feet to a second-story window of our city hall. I notified an official, who seemed shocked, but nothing was done, and a year later the vine had spread farther. I called attention to it again, but nothing happened. At the beginning of the third season, I apparently reached the right man. When next I looked, the beautiful green leaves were all dead.[1]

For the most part, other "poisonous plants" are only so when eaten. A cardinal rule is *never* to chew on anything unless you have checked it out and are certain that you recognize it as harmless. This is especially true of fungi such as mushrooms and toadstools. There are several supposed ways of telling the poisonous from the edible, handed down from pioneer days. Not one of these methods is safe to use.

We are surrounded on all sides by plants poisonous to eat. Young children must be watched to see that they don't chew on greenery unknown to the parent, or even on recognized plants not known to be poisonous. The leaf stems of rhubarb are used for sauce, but were you to eat the leaf blades you would sicken and probably die.

Do not eat the seed inside a peach, apricot, or cherry pit; it contains hydrocyanic acid. A man who loved to eat apple seeds once saved them until he had a cupful. Then he ate them all at once and died, perhaps from cyanide poisoning.

The common yew, widely used as an ornamental shrub, is highly poisonous if eaten; so are the bulbs of snowdrops, daffodils, and some others.

Castor-bean seeds are so poisonous that if a person swallows several of them, death usually follows. From pressing the seeds, ordinary castor oil is made. It is not poisonous because the poison itself is not soluble in oil.

Do not chew on a horse-chestnut seed; besides tasting awful, it is poisonous. One author says that the seeds, crushed and presumably cooked, make a good paste—one that will repel chewing insects found in libraries.

Notice that all the above plants are usually associated with civilization. Now for a few found in the wild (but not always exclusively). Cherry trees, except for the fruit, contain hydrocyanic acid combined with various sugars. Wilting or digestion of the leaves helps to release the poison. Livestock are often killed by browsing on cherry foliage fresh or wilted; the wild black cherry tree has the highest cyanide concentration of any of the common cherries.

Every day of our lives we eat food that contains very small amounts of numerous preservatives and other additives, perhaps any of which would kill us if taken in large enough amounts. There is a relation between the lethal quantity of a poison and body weight. Enough to kill a young child might be tolerated by an adult.

Oak acorns are classified as "poisonous," but this needs explaining. The poisonous ingredient is tannin, readily soluble in hot water. Oaks are grouped into "whites" and "reds." The latter have so much tannin that they are not edible. But white-oak acorns are relatively sweet, with just small amounts of tannin. Even so, it is very tedious to boil out enough of the tannin to make them edible.

The Indians, after removing the outer shells, pounded the dried acorn kernels with a mortar and pestle into meal or flour. This was spread over the bottom of a closely woven basket or other filter. Hot water was trickled through until it no longer showed the brown tannin color. Or, the meal was stirred in hot water in a container. After the meal settled, the brownish tannin solution was poured off, and the process was repeated until the water was no longer tannin brown. The meal was then formed into cakes and baked in hot ashes or primitive ovens. Not only was acorn meal or flour an important food for many tribes of AmerIndians, but there are references to its use among the ancient peoples of Europe. An English writer of the 1600s stated that before the discovery of "corn" (wheat), acorns were the food of men, nay of Jupiter himself, and men indeed had hearts of oak.

Jack-in-the-Pulpit has an underground bulb known as Indian-turnip. Some people in the know have invited the neophyte to sample a slice of the raw bulb—I speak from an experience of long ago. At first there is no warning, as you munch the sample, of the agony to follow. Then the entire mucous membrane of mouth and throat begins to burn most horribly, and continues to do so for several hours. It was thought that needle-shaped crystals of calcium oxalate found in the cells actually pierced the mouth and throat lining. Recent work suggests that an enzyme is responsible. In any case, boiling does not destroy the effect, but baking does. However, the core may still be incompletely cooked. It is better to peel the green bulb and cut it into very thin slices. Spread them out, and allow them to dry in the sun for a week or so until they are crisp. They can then be ground into an edible flour, and dried further if any sting remains. In most places, "Jacks" are not common enough to warrant destroying them.[2]

POISONOUS PLANTS

1. Page 112—Send for a copy of the U.S. Department of Agriculture's Bulletin No. 1972, "Poison Ivy, Poison Oak, and Poison Sumac." Superintendent of Documents, U.S. Government Printing Office, Washington, D.C. 20402 (10¢). Methods of eradication are given along with important details that are omitted in my short account.

2. Page 113—I give only a few examples of poisonous plants, gleaned in part from John M. Kingsbury's monumental *Poisonous Plants of the United States and Canada*. Englewood Cliffs, NJ: Prentice-Hall, 1964. This 6,000-page book lists some 1,700 references. Although primarily for livestock farmers, the book also covers the effects of plant poisons on humans. A copy of the book should be in every camp and school library.

BLOODSUCKING AND STINGING PESTS

Mosquitoes

"I never saw the muskitoes more plentiful in any part of America than they are here [in New York State]. They are so eager for our blood that we could not rest all the night, though we surrounded ourselves with fire."

These words were penned in 1771 by Peter Kalm, one of the early explorer-botanists. They are just as true now as they were then.[1] It would be easy to write a horror story about these tiny but formidable critters. Although I shall try to do no such thing, you should respect them, and be prepared to defend yourself from their attacks. They can cause great misery, and completely ruin your camping trip or exploration in the outdoors.

To most people a mosquito is a mosquito, but there are several hundred kinds scattered around the world. New York State alone has about 53 different species. All but five attack humans. Some mosquitoes attack any warmblooded land animal that walks, flies, or swims. Others are more choosy and go after only coldblooded animals such as turtles, frogs, and snakes. But these whining mini-demons all have two things in common: they need standing water to breed, and only the female "bites" (actually pierces). The male is an unobtrusive fellow who feeds on plant juices or nothing at all. In most cases, a feeding of blood is needed by the female so that her eggs will hatch and develop.

You and your campers might scoop up with a glass container some stagnant water containing mosquito "wigglers" (larvae). Look through the side of the glass and notice that every few seconds each larva comes to the surface to breathe. If you place a drop of oil on the water, the larvae soon suffocate—they can't get through the oil for oxygen. This is the basis for most mosquito control. Now pour out the water, wipe away any traces of oil, and replace the larvae. Over several days' time, you can watch the transformation of larva to pupa. (The four stages are egg, larva, pupa, and adult.) The pupa rests on the water surface, and the mature mosquito emerges from a crack along its back. One time at Sargent Camp, the girls brought into the dining hall an aquarium filled with water and several hundred mosquito larvae for observation. They forgot to cover it with netting. Several days later there was an "unexplained" plague of mosquitoes!

As you travel either north or south from the approximate latitudes of New York State, the mosquito population tends to increase. Especially in the far north, during the short summer, innumerable shallow pools breed untold billions of the winged harpies. They settle in clouds on wildlife, man, and his domestic animals. Thousands of animals—wild and domestic—may be killed. An unprepared human, especially a child, can be made physically sick and driven to the edge of madness by their around-the-clock attacks. It might seem strange that such an insignificant insect easily crushed between thumb and forefinger could be so dangerous. It's the almost infinite number of them that's so deadly. Happily, most of the time you will never have such an experience, unless you travel during the warm months in places well-known for these flying pests.

It will satisfy most people just to protect themselves with one of the popular bug dopes, such as Cutters, or others containing N, N diethyl-meta-toluamide. I recall my first experience with this repellent. I drove to the edge of a mosquito-infested swamp. With both arms bared to the elbow, I applied a small amount of the repellent to the left arm only. I extended both arms and waited—but not for long. In came the mosquitoes, hungry for my blood. About a half-dozen settled on my right arm and began to feed. I paid them no attention. My gaze was focused on the treated left arm. It seemed as though a whole fleet of miniature fighter planes came zooming in to attack. But perhaps an inch or two from my arm they seemed to hit an invisible barrier, and turned away. Not one landed!

I might leave this whole subject right here, but I must let you know about an article by R. H. Wright, "Why Mosquito Repellents Repel."[2] He wrote: "I supposed a mosquito 'likes' the smell of the hosts and 'dislikes' the smell of a repellent... The experiments I shall describe show that this naive view is completely wrong." In general (species behavior varies), if you have a hundred or so mosquitoes in a screened cage and pipe in carbon-dioxide gas, they become more active and start exploring. If there are three targets, one warm, one moist, and the third both warm and moist, a few mosquitoes fly to the warm one. More go to the wet one. The overwhelming horde is drawn to the warm, wet target. Special photography shows that our bodies do indeed give off a continuous cloak of warm, moist air. The continuous stream of carbon dioxide from our lungs notifies each mosquito within range that dinner's on the table. She then just zooms in and finds the layer of warm, moist air around us. And what does the repellent do? Apparently its molecules, as they leave our bodies, block the mosquito's warmth and moisture sensors in the antennae. When the mosquito flies into the edge of the repellent zone, it cannot detect our warm, moist aura, and so it turns away.

This research—here only briefly described—covered a number of years of experimentation. It shows again that whenever we look into a seemingly simple facet of nature, we usually find unimagined complexity.

More than 25,000 organic substances have been tested as repellents. Many of the recently developed chemicals are far more effective than the earlier ones so widely used. To get the same repellency with old-fashioned citronellol as with that of diethyl toluamide, there must be a concentration in the air 1,000 times greater!

Mosquitoes, along with other bloodsucking flies, seem to be attracted by certain colors. One of these is blue—so much for blue jeans and the visually polluting blue tents scattered through the woods.

Blackflies

Like the mosquitoes, blackflies are found world-wide; with more than 600 species, they are major pests. Unlike mosquitoes, blackflies breed only in fast-running streams, attack only in daylight, and have a relatively short season of about two months. In the central Adirondacks, this runs from about May 15 to July 15. June is blackfly month—a good time to stay away from the woods, unless you're a dedicated fisherman or you must be there for some other reason.

At their worst, especially along streams, blackflies are almost unbearable. Clouds of them swarm around your head. They crawl into your hair, ears, nostrils, and even your mouth—if you open it. An open collar is an invitation to dinner—eagerly accepted! Up your pants legs and shirt sleeves they go. In fact, there's no place on your body they won't find—and bite. In the December 1976 issue of the Canadian Geographical Journal, Fred Gaskin tells how he met a cloud of blackflies of "plague proportion" while exploring northern Canada. Within a few seconds of the attack, his shirt and trousers "appeared to be covered by a deep layer of thick black fur." Only his head net and insect repellent "saved" him, perhaps literally.

In most cases, the bite of the blackfly is painless. You don't even notice it as you try in vain to shoo the flies away from your face. Unlike mosquito bites, those of the blackfly female keep oozing blood, after she has gorged herself and flown to the nearest brook to lay her eggs—hundreds of them at one sitting. Meantime, the bites on you begin to swell, redden, and itch. This may continue for days or weeks. Scratching worsens the situation by promoting skin infections.

Although certain people may tolerate being bitten, others—especially children—are often seriously affected by receiving too many bites. They even may have "blackfly fever," with excessively swollen faces, headache, nausea, and swollen, tender lymph nodes in the neck. In common with mosquitoes, blackflies in sufficient numbers kill domestic and wild animals. The blood from bites in the nostrils tends to make breathing difficult. The victim then resorts to mouth-breathing. The flies crawl inside and may bite around the base of the tongue, which swells enough to stop the passage of air. The animal dies of suffocation.

Nowadays you'll try to protect yourself with a contact toluamide repellent on face, neck, and hands. Lower concentrations in aerosol cans are applied to trouser bottoms and shirt sleeves. You'll find in Kephart many recipes for bug dope as it used to be made.[3] We didn't care how messy it was, or how we smelled to other people, as long as it protected us—which it did, more or less.

Old Nessmuk, with his 40 years' experience in the Adirondack wilderness nearly a century ago, published his favorite formula in Forest and Stream: "Three ounces of pine tar, two of castor oil, and one of pennyroyal oil. Simmer together over a 'slow fire' and bottle for use." To apply, he wrote, "Rub it in thoroughly and liberally at first, and after you have established a good glaze...don't fool with soap and towels. A coat of this varnish grows better the longer it is kept on—and it is cleanly and wholesome." On a seven-week trip, he boasted, he didn't surrender to any "weak whim connected with soap and water." When he reached a woodland hotel, he washed up and found that his skin not only had a "ruddy tanned look" but was also "very soft and smooth ... In fact as a lotion for the skin it is excellent. It is a soothing and healing application for poisonous bites already received."[4]

For many years at our Adirondack Forestry Camp, we developed an additional defense against flies and mosquitoes. After applying our favorite dope (pine tar wasn't popular), we buttoned and turned up our collars. The edge of a large handkerchief (preferably silk) was passed around the base of the collar and tied in front. The opposite edge was brought up over the head and the ends tied over the forehead. With hat on, nothing but the face was exposed. This rig kept most of the blackflies from crawling around and into the ears.

All things come to an end, and by the first week in July the worst is usually over. At this time, if you look closely at a blackfly you may see that it has white "stockings" on its feet. The lumberjacks said that the flies were getting old, hence the white feet. Actually, the white denotes another species that hatches toward the end of the season.

Because of climatic differences as you climb a mountain, the blackfly season is often in August at the higher elevations. Be prepared.

Until recent times, the blackfly ruined June as a tourist month in the woods. Now, a selective larvicide is used in streams near resort areas, and you may not see a single fly during your visit. Also, large populations may have a limited spread. Blackflies may be very bad in one place and hardly noticed 10 miles away. Their activity is also influenced by the weather. Muggy, warm to hot day brings them out in full force.

Punkies (biting midges, no-see-ums)

"The most troublesome plague to both man and beast, especially in passing through the woods, was a kind of insect called by the Indian, Ponk, or *Living Ashes,* from their being so small that they are hardly visible, and their bite as painful as the burning of red-hot ashes."—Loskiel, 1794

Outdoor writers differ on the painfulness of the bite. I cannot quite agree with the above description. They can be bad, but to me the severity of a single bite takes third place to that of either mosquito or blackfly. Of course, if some 300 punkies land on your arm and start feeding, all within two minutes, you may feel as though your arm is on fire, sure enough.

My first experience caused as much astonishment as it did pain. I suddenly began to feel needle-pricks on my arms, face, and neck. It was dusk. I looked carefully at my bare arms: the failing light showed nothing to explain what was happening. I quickly took out my hand lens and looked again. There they were, dozens of them—tiny critters that hardly seemed big enough (being just one-tenth of an inch long) to drive their "stilettos" into the human epidermis. One hard sweep of the hand crushed them, but others took their places. Not only are they almost invisible—you can't hear them either.

Like woodland mosquitoes, punkies are sensitive to a lack of moisture in the air. During the day, they're usually not troublesome unless you're in moist, shaded woodlands. They come out at dusk, and are attracted to light. Passing through ordinary window screens as though they weren't there, punkies may attack people inside cottages and camps.

Unlike either mosquitoes or blackflies, punkies breed in moist places such as wet leaves, or along fallen, decaying tree trunks. They are most numerous in June and July, and by the middle of

August there are few left. Any protective screening you use along with a good repellent must be as tightly woven as cheesecloth.

Deerflies

A smaller relative of the horsefly, the deerfly nonetheless is huge compared to the three above-mentioned insect demons—and so is its bite! It will follow you patiently along the trail and even hitch a ride on the brim of your felt hat. If you're foolish enough not to wear a hat, a deerfly will crawl into your hair and bite. Then when you run your fingers through your hair, they may come out smeared with your blood! Fortunately, deerflies are relatively few in number, and they are slow, clumsy flyers. However, when one lands on your bare skin, you'd better crush it at once. If you give it a chance to bite, you'll be sorry.

Some Comfort

Admittedly, the foregoing descriptions, compressed into a few words and read at one sitting, may make you despair of hiking or camping in the woods during fly-time. But there's great variability between different areas, time of day, temperature and humidity, and whether or not control measures are used locally against mosquitoes and blackflies. Just be sure you're prepared for the worst, and the sunlit greenwood may still work its magic in your soul.[5]

BLOODSUCKING AND STINGING PESTS

1. Page 114—There are many publications on insect pests. One of the best is Hugo Jamnback's *Bloodsucking Flies and Other Outdoor Nuisance Arthropods of New York State.* Memoir 19, State Museum, Albany, NY. See also A. LaBastille, "The Black Fly," *Adirondack Life Magazine,* Summer 1974, pp. 10-12.

2. Page 115—R.H. Wright, "Why Mosquito Repellents Repel." *Scientific American,* No. 233, July 1975, pp. 104-111.

3. Page 116—Horace Kephart, *Camping and Woodcraft.* New York: NJ: Macmillan, 1972.

4. Page 116—Nessmuk (G.W. Sears), *Woodcraft.* New York: Dover Publications, 1963.

5. Page 117—It is not my intent to catalog all the pests you might meet in any part of North America. To find more about chiggers (red-bugs), write for "Controlling Chiggers," Home and Garden Bulletin No. 137. Agricultural Research Service, U.S. Department of Agriculture, Washington, DC. 1976. Chiggers and ticks are covered by Hugo Jamnback (see note for page 183, above).

   See also J.A. Wilkerson, *Medicine for Mountaineering.* Seattle, WA: The Mountaineers, 1975. This book should be in every camper's library. It gives specific treatment for insect and scorpion stings, and bites caused by spiders, snakes, and other wild animals. Also see R.E. Arnold, *What To Do About Bites and Stings of Venomous Animals.* New York: Macmillan, 1973. The book has 122 pages, 77 of them on reptiles. Thirty-four pages list the sources of antivenins.

   It is beyond the scope of this book to discuss the serious worldwide impact of insect-borne diseases.

FORESTRY IN SUMMER CAMPS

Even though many camps are surrounded by trees, and the forest offers human values and pursuits not to be found anywhere else, these benefits are often overlooked by the average camp director and his staff. For most camps the woods are just a green backdrop for tennis courts, ball diamonds, and the like. These may have their place, but why neglect the priceless woodland experiences—the flash of blue-jay wings, the sun's rays streaming down through the green tree tops far overhead, the music of the wind, the song of a crystal-clear woodland brook and the feel of its cool running water swirling around your bare feet, or the great silences heard only when one listens? These and countless other forest gifts are the birthright of every boy and girl. But they need interpreters. Do you enjoy exploring wood-

land trails? Do you like adventuring with map and compass? Do you recognize the various trees and greet them as friends?

If you now glance back quickly at the title of this section, you may wonder whether we are on the right trail! But what is "forestry"? Is it just the growing of trees for sawlogs and pulpwood, keeping trees on steep watersheds to prevent erosion, or fighting wildfires in the woods? These are some of the traditional things that concern foresters. But a new day is here. The Yale School of Forestry is now the School of Forestry and Environmental Studies, and the New York State College of Forestry is State University of New York College of Environmental Science and Forestry. The long-term problems of producing good sawlogs are complex enough. But a much greater challenge is to understand and try to manage the *whole environment* for the best interests of the human race. This, of course, is applied ecology—the "ec" is from a Greek word meaning "house"; and "ology" means "the study of." Ecology, then, is the study of our house—the whole planet— what it does for us and what we do for or to it. The basic effort of the discipline is to try to understand the ways in which all the world's plants and animals interact with each other and their environment. This poses innumerable problems so awesome that we may never solve them all. But perhaps enough can be understood and acted upon to prevent the doom of the family of man.

So now, what would you like to do with your forest, and how can campers get involved? On my trip to 30 children's camps to see whether forestry projects could be started (see Preface), I found at one camp a crowded stand of pole-size white pine. The crowns met overhead, slowing tree growth. With compass and measuring tape we laid out and staked a rectangle 120 feet by 60 feet. This gave us two plots, 60 × 60. One we left as a control. We "operated" on the other. First we cut down the dead, the dying, and the cripples—those with one or more sharp bends in the trunk. The remaining trees were the co-dominants, which formed most of the canopy, and the few dominants that in the fierce competition had won by growing faster and getting their heads above the general level. In our forest, some of the co-dominants had to go to make room for those remaining. At this point, it takes an expert to do a good job of selection, but for the purpose in view, you and your campers can do well enough. When thinning of the stand was completed, each tree's crown of green needles had about four or five feet of space all around, between it and its neighbors. Finally, with hand saws lubricated with kerosene, we cut off the lower dead branches close to the trunk. Since branches become knots in boards cut from a tree, the new growth each year, after pruning, would be clear of knots. Although this is forestry treatment for growing select clear white pine, doesn't such a stand look better aesthetically? For the effect of this practice upon growth, see Fig. 44.

What we did would apply to a dense young natural stand of conifers, to a plantation where the spacing might be 6 × 6 feet, and to a broadleaf forest. In dense evergreen forests, the ground may have a thick layer of dead needles, and only a few weeds can be seen. Flocks of starlings and other birds often roost there in great numbers year after year. The seeds of various kinds of fruits pass through their digestive tracts and rain down in untold thousands. Many of the seeds remain dormant, covered over by layer after layer of needles. When the stand is thinned, the trees begin to grow faster, not only because their green needles get more light but also—very importantly—because root competition for water and minerals is much reduced. Then too, when the thinnings are dragged out, the needles are tumbled, and dormant seeds germinate in the moist earth underneath. Within two years, you may have a jungle of wild grapes, elders, cherries, poison-ivy, Virginia creeper, sumac, nightshade, buckthorn, and others. All these were brought in by the birds—an excellent example of ecology! It should be said that such a sequence is most common in planted, thinned evergreen forests on heavy clay soils that previously supported broadleaf trees. In mountain-ous and/or sandy regions where conifers naturally predominate, it is perhaps more likely that their own seeds begin a new generation of softwoods. But even here, hardwoods often follow softwoods.

You may have some areas where a dense stand of young hardwoods is reaching upward. Here is an excellent chance to favor the more important trees such as sugar maple, yellow birch, black cherry, white oak, white ash, tuliptree (yellow poplar), basswood, black walnut, and certain hickories. Just enough weeding can be done to liberate the few fine, straight, fast-growing young trees. Tag the good trees with colored ribbon. Campers and staff have fun cutting away the competition, and will get great satisfaction year after year in seeing how their liberated trees grow and prosper.

Perhaps you have an abandoned farm with open fields, part of which you might reforest. This, of course, should be done in spring before growth starts, or in autumn after growth has ceased and the rains have once again moistened the earth. Your state forestry or conservation department will send you a list of available trees, in most cases ever-greens.

Miss Laura Mattoon, for many years director of Camp Kehonka, N.H. told me how she once ordered 1,000 pines and spruces for spring planting. She worried some about transporting such a large number of trees from the railroad station several miles away. Finally the great day arrived; the camp truck and station wagon along with Miss Mattoon in her own car, made up the caravan. She figured they could make several trips if necessary. At the express office she announced proudly, "I've come for my thousand trees." Imagine her astonishment when the agent handed her one small package, perhaps two feet long and a foot in diameter.

"There must be some mistake; there can't be a thousand trees in there."

"Waal, that's all there is." She took the pack-age, and on the way back to camp she composed in her mind the letter of outrage she would send to the state tree nursery—after she had seen what was in the package. When she opened it and saw how small and closely packed the trees were, she began to sim-mer down and think that perhaps she hadn't been cheated. By the time they got the trees all planted, they were sure there must have been a thousand of them, even without counting!

Some 50 years later I told this story to our college's experiment-station director. He smiled and said, "A few people still bring a truck or trailer for a couple hundred trees."

Now, how will you space your trees? I hope you won't blanket the field with monotonous 6 × 6-foot spacing. How about planting them in scattered groups of 50 to 100 or so, with patches of meadow in between? Or, perhaps you'd like to use an open field to plant closely spaced conifers in a strip 10 to 15 feet wide and 75 to 100 feet long, oriented exactly north-south. At the north end, the strip would ter-minate in an arrowhead. Partway down you would plant a "crossbar" of trees perpendicular to your long strip. A separate planting in the shape of an "N" just north of the arrow would complete the design— a very interesting and useful display from the air. On one English estate, a tree pattern forms an enormous ace of clubs!

Are there some good broadleaf trees already started? You might develop a mixed stand. Also, don't forget the birds and other animals. From the Soil Conservation Service (see your county agent) you can get various species of shrubs and trees that bear fruit attractive to wildlife. These species can be spot-planted throughout the plantation.

Before you leave camp in the fall, be sure to walk over the site you expect to plant next spring. If the field has only short grasses and weeds, you are in luck. Is it densely covered with bracken fern knee-high, or other weeds waist-high? If so, you have a problem. After winter snows have flattened the weeds, the field may look like a perfect place to plant, but by early summer the weeds will have over-topped the little trees. Unless liberated, many or most of them may die. Can you enthuse your campers and staff to the point where they will help you weed, or do you have camp labor to call upon? (Don't forget Mark Twain's Tom Sawyer.) Also re-member that in many states you can get advice on tree planting from the district forester. Properly or-ganized forestry projects for camps and schools are fun for the kids. And they're of great value in help-ing everyone to better understand the natural en-vironment that unfortunately is so foreign to the average city dweller.[1]

It used to be thought that every forestry col-lege graduate should know by experience how to plant trees. Fig. 45 shows part of my freshman-year class establishing a forest plantation on a worn-out piece of abandoned farmland. Originally cleared of forest by hardy pioneers, the land produced crops until the blanket of humus was exhausted—only sterile sand and rocks remained underneath.

We were excused from classes for a week. It was beautiful spring weather; the birds were singing. We camped out and were fed by a lumberjack cook. We weren't paid, but it never occurred to us that we were being exploited. We had a great time!

When we packed up to leave, I never thought I'd see the place again, but fate kept me at the college for all of my professional life, and over the years, I visited the growing plantation several times. Finally, 50 years after it had been planted, I visited it once more. Fig. 45 (bottom) shows what changes Time had made. The largest trees were 16 inches in diameter. It gave me a great thrill.

So I say to you all, PLANT TREES. The younger you start the better, but at any age it's still worthwhile to plant something that may be flour-ishing a century or more after you've gone. Five years ago, I planted a young tuliptree in our front yard. Even now, it's nearly 20 feet tall; in time, with its arrow-straight trunk, it could grow into a mag-nificent tree more than 100 feet tall and five feet in diameter. Only trees that grow in the open form their distinctive crown shape. The lower branches of crowded forest trees compete with each other for light, and when the shade becomes too deep, these lower branches die and fall off. In time, the lower trunk becomes clear.

Apparently, when most people plant trees around their homes, they never think about doing any pruning. Myself, I like to see broadleaf trees with an imposing trunk some 10 feet to the first branch. On small trees, pruning is done gradually— the lowest branch first, the next year the one above, and so on. When people do prune their trees, they often leave short stubs sticking out. *Never* do this! It invites decay. The tree cannot properly grow wood and bark over these ends. On older trees with large branches, you do make an undercut, out about six inches from the trunk, and then saw through from the top. This prevents a heavy branch from tearing away some of the bark and wood underneath it when it falls. But then the stub must be sawed off flush with the trunk.

Perhaps you'll consider "protecting" the raw wood surface with paint. It's useless. Tiny cracks de-velop that trap the microscopic spores of wood-decaying fungi. For some reason, I don't like to see white scars staring at me from the dark tree trunk, so I carefully brush on Tree Coat, trying to cover just the wood. You can buy it at nursery stores. These chemicals are not helpful to live cambial and inner-bark tissues, however.

Recently, a tree pathologist was asked about these coatings. He smiled and said, "They probably do the person brushing them on more good than they do the tree." If they are to give any protection, each year you must inspect the surface; if drying cracks have developed, brush on more of the coat-ing. Drainage is the most important thing, however. There mustn't be places where water can stand and keep the wound moist.

Besides pruning the lower branches, you may want to thin out the crown, especially on trees that are shade-tolerant and produce many closely spaced branches. Where a branch rubs against another one, the bark may be worn away, opening the tree to de-

Fig. 44: Cross section of a pine tree. Note increasingly slower growth
due to crowding, then the enormous increase in growth after thinning.
(From Inside Wood by W.M. Harlow.)

cay. Each autumn after the leaves have fallen, study the branch patterns and decide whether or not you can improve the tree's appearance—pruning is an art. Most people just let their shade trees grow wild for many years. Then when they get too big, a "woodbutcher" is hired to make the trees smaller. He just saws off a lot of the top and side branches, leaving long stubs two to four inches in diameter—a horrible sight!

You can get needed information on tree planting from many sources, including your own state conservation department. Remember that a tree out of the ground is like a fish out of water. You should feel very uneasy about those hundreds of rootlets until they are safely back in their home element. They must not be exposed to the sun or wind, even for a few minutes, and at all times they must be kept moist—preferably covered with wet burlap or dunked in a bucket of water.

FORESTRY IN SUMMER CAMPS

1. Page 120—See Leon S. Minckler, *Woodland Ecology: Environmental Forestry for the Small Landowner.* Syracuse, NY: Syracuse University Press, 1975. Dr. Minckler is Professor Emeritus of our college. His delightfully written and beautifully illustrated book should be in every camp and school library in the eastern United States.

Fig. 45: 1) Crew of forestry students planting white pines on an old field, 1922. 2) Author stands in resulting forest, 1972. Largest trees are 16 inches in diameter.

PEOPLE-WILDERNESS POSTSCRIPT

How thousands of people can experience wilderness without loving it to death poses enormous and varying problems. In this vast country of ours, there are many kinds of wild lands, each with its own local concerns. Some of these concerns may be quite different from those in an area 100 miles away—to say nothing of 1,000 miles or more. Other problems are universal.

I'm bemused at the completely contradictory and sometimes impractical advice given by authors of equal stature. A famous outdoor club tells you to "conceal" fish offal back a ways from a stream or lake. The delicious aroma of fish will attract coons, mink, skunks, and others from quite some distance—depending upon wind flow. Even after animals have feasted, the spot will smell fishy. If you're

thinking of burying, forget it. The little animals' sense of smell is acute. They'll dig up the mess anyway. How much better is it to follow the trout and salmon fisherman's habit? Upon catching a fish, he immediately cuts out the guts and drops them into the stream where they are soon snapped up and returned to the aquatic food chain. Unfortunately, too many fishermen are careless and leave a bloody mess on shore alongside the stream, where they dress their entire catch.

Certainly a major problem is what to do with human feces. Suppose there is a camping area large enough so that three groups of 10 each (more is an abomination) can settle in out of sight and sound of each other. In a two-month summer season, that will total 1,800 humans to be serviced! A prestigious outdoor club recommends the "cat-hole" method, as though it were something new. But thousands of years ago, the Mosaic Law required this very method to be used by the Israelites during their nomadic wanderings. Deuteronomy 23, 13-15 states:

"Thou shalt have a place also without the camp, whither thou shalt go forth abroad. And thou shalt have a paddle among thy weapons; and it shall be, when thou sittest down abroad, thou shalt dig therewith, and shalt turn back and cover that which cometh from thee. For the Lord thy God walketh in the midst of thy camp."

This seems to be an excellent method for a few people. But how about when the season's population approaches 2,000 or more? The forest floor will look as though it had the measles! Oh yes, you're supposed to completely back-fill the hole and landscape it with the ground-cover plants you carefully removed. When you leave, it may look good, but in most cases the plants soon die.

What to do? A slit trench for the group should be dug; some say six to eight inches deep, others eight to 18. The idea is to be within the layer of soil where bacterial action is the quickest. Depending on some unknown variables, this is probably not much more than 10 inches down. In many places, you'll be lucky if you can go that deep without hitting large tree roots or rocks. When the trench is filled with dirt and camouflaged, what's to prevent the digger in the next group from saying, "That looks like a good place for a latrine." An unpleasant surprise waits! The U.S. Army solved this problem a long time ago. They leave a small marker labelled "Latrine filled on (date)." Will we need to do some

124

such thing in the most heavily used wilderness areas?

Some hikers, for one-time use, just turn over a partly buried rock and, having deposited, roll the rock back into place. Although this is acceptable in some places, anyone who does this where rocks are scarce or the place is a much-used camping area is setting up a most unpleasant experience for the next visitor who comes along with the same idea!

No matter what method of disposal is used, a well-known hiking club says: "Latrines should be located at least 50 yards from any camping area, stream, lake or dry stream course." The U.S. Forest Service agrees with this rule. But if the advice is followed to the letter, I leave you to imagine where the highest concentrations will be, depending on the terrain. I advise a *minimum* of 100 feet. Like some other rules under the wilderness "museum" concept, this is an open-ended question. Among other conditions, soil porosity makes a big difference. And, of course, nearly everything depends on how many users are involved within short periods of time.

Besides backpacking, there are many other important ways of experiencing and enjoying the wilderness. Basically, I would hope that all children might have the kind of experience found in L.B. Sharp's decentralized camps. There the emphasis is not just in travelling *through* the wilderness, but rather upon living, in small groups, surrounded *by* the wilderness. The forest keeps growing more than enough firewood, and furnishes all sorts of craft materials. The campers slowly absorb the essential lore of their primitive heritage, and develop skills that cannot be learned in a few days, even though the leadership is excellent. I hope that many more millions of our children and adults may be adding such experiences to their memory store. Time, the Great Mystery, bears us all along.

I would like to close with the prophetic words of William Gray, written long ago.

"The evening campfire of our lives burns low, and the shadows, with stealthy approach, close around us. We dispel them with a bit of the crystalized sunshine of other days, a memory which blazes us, as does this rib of an ancient and forgotten pine; but it, too, dims to a coal, and fades to ashes. There is a sigh of a passing breeze in the pines, the note of a distant night bird—whatever is heard amid the prevailing silence is gentle and soothing."[1]

PEOPLE-WILDERNESS POSTSCRIPT

1. Page 125—The end quotation is from a very old pamphlet, probably printed privately. I could find no more information on it.

SOME SELECTED REFERENCES

"Of making many books there is no end, and much study is a weariness of the flesh." Ecclesiastes 12:12, written when "books" were handwritten scrolls.

This list of references includes those to which I've referred in the text, and a few others. It's just a sample of the vast amount of literature on the wild outdoors. In reading the old classics such as Nessmuk and Kephart you'll find many practices no longer allowable to the backpacker or canoeist in specified wilderness areas. (However, everyone should read Nessmuk's little book for its charming style, and to get some idea of the great American wilderness of a century ago.) In some of the more recent books especially, there are some serious errors. But never mind, you'll soon discover them when you begin to explore the outdoors and develop your own ways of doing things. After all, books are only springboards to help you attain total immersion in the natural world—an achievement that takes years and years of experience.

For a list of many outdoors books, be sure to get the Backpacker Books Catalog No. 5, Main Street, Orwell, VT 05760. 67 pp. 1978.

American Camping Association. Campcraft Instructors' Manual. Martinsville, IN 46151. 1973.

American Camping Association. 1977 Catalog of Selected Camping Publications.

American National Red Cross. Standard First Aid and Personal Safety. Doubleday, Garden City, NY. 268 pp. 1976.

Angier, Bradford. How to Stay Alive in the Woods, Macmillan, New York, NY. 285 pp. 1972.

Arnold, Richard E. What To Do About Bites and Stings of Venomous Animals. Macmillan, New York, NY. 122 pp. 1973.

Battan, Lovis J. Weather. Prentice-Hall Englewood Cliffs, NJ. 136 pp. 1974.

Brown, Vinson. Knowing the Outdoors in the Dark. Stackpole Books, Harrisburg, PA. 191 pp. 1972.

Conway, Steve. Timber Cutting Practices. Miller Freeman, San Francisco, CA. 192 pp. 1973.

Coon, Nelson. Using Wayside Plants. Hearthside Press, New York, NY. 1969.

Davidson, James West and John Rugge. The Complete Wilderness Paddler. Alfred A. Knopf, New York, NY. 259 pp. 1975.

Densmore, Frances. How Indians Used Wild Plants for Food, Medicine, and Crafts. Dover, New York, NY. 397 pp. 1974. (Originally published as "Uses of Plants by the Chippewa Indians," 44th Annual Report of the Bureau of American Ethnology, Washington DC, 1926-27.)

Dover is well known for its republication of the older classics, including those on the outdoors. Although the prices are modest, its paperbacks are of superior quality; sewn in signatures like more expensive books, they can be opened flat, and have years of service in them. Send for the catalog. Dover Publications, 180 Varick St., New York, NY. 10014.

Disley, John. Your Way with Map and Compass. (Teacher's book.) Silva Co., LaPorte, IN 46350. 61 pp. 1973.

Disley, John. Orienteering. (Student's book. See above listing.) 32 pp.

Fear, G. Surviving the Unexpected Wilderness Emergency. Survival Education Association, Tacoma, WA. 192 pp. 1975.

Fleming, June. The Well-Fed Backpacker. Victoria House, Portland, OR. 96 pp. 1976.

Fletcher, Colin. The New Complete Walker. Alfred A. Knopf, New York, NY. 353 pp. 1974.

Goodrich, Lois. Decentralized Camping. Association Press, New York, NY. 256 pp. 1959. (Out of print).

Hall, Alan. The Wild Food Trailguide. Holt, Rinehart, and Winston, New York, NY. 230 pp. 1976.

Harlow, William M. Trees of the Eastern and Central United States and Canada. Dover, New York, NY. 288 pp. 1957.

Harlow, William M. Inside Wood, Masterpiece of Nature. The American Forestry Association, Washington, DC. 120 pp. 1970.

Hart, John. Walking Softly in the Wilderness. Sierra Club Books, San Francisco, CA. 436 pp. 1977.

Jaeger, Ellsworth. Wildwood Wisdom. Macmillan, New York, NY. 491 pp. 1945.

Kauffman, Henry J. American Axes. Stephen Greene Press, Brattlesboro, VT. 151 pp. 1972.

Kelsey, Robert. Walking in the Wild: The Complete Guide to Hiking and Backpacking. Funk and Wagnalls, New York, NY. 362 pp. 1973.

Kemsley, William Jr. and the Editors of Backpacker Magazine. Backpacking Equipment Buyer's Guide. Collier MacMillan, New York, NY. 285 pp. 1977.

Kephart, Horace. Camping and Woodcraft. Macmillan, Riverside, NJ. 1972.

Kingsbury, John M. Poisonous Plants of the United States and Canada. Prentice-Hall, Englewood Cliffs, NJ. 6,000 pp. 1964.

Kjellström, Björn. Be Expert with Map and Compass. Charles Scribner's Sons, New York, NY. 136 pp. 1967.

Laubin, Reginald and Gladys. The Indian Tipi. University of Oklahoma Press, Norman, OK. 350 pp. 1977.

Lee, Albert. Weather Wisdom. Dolphin Books (Doubleday), New York, NY. 1977.

Leopold, Aldo. A Sand County Almanac, and Sketches Here and There. Oxford University Press, New York, NY. 266 pp. 1974.

Manning, Harvey. Backpacking: One Step at a Time. R.E.I. Press, Seattle, WA. 351 pp. 1972.

Marshall, Mel. Cooking Over Coals. Winchester Press, New York, NY. 314 pp. 1971.

Mason, Bernard Sterling. Woodcraft and Camping. Dover, New York, NY. 580 pp. 1974. (Originally published as Woodcraft, A.S. Barnes, 1939.)

Medsger, Oliver Perry. Edible Wild Plants. MacMillan, New York, NY. 1966.

Melham, Tom. John Muir's Wild America. National Geographic Society, Washington, DC. 200 pp. 1976.

Miller, Warren. Crosscut Saw Manual. U.S. Forest Service Equipment Development Center, Missoula, MT 59807. 27 pp. 1977.

Mills, Enos A. Wild Life on the Rockies. Houghton Mifflin, Boston, MA. 257 pp. 1922.

Minckler, Leon Sherwood. Woodland Ecology: Environmental Forestry for the Small Landowner. Syracuse University Press, Syracuse, NY. 1975.

Nessmuk (George Washington Sears). Woodcraft. Dover, New York, NY. 105 pp. 1963. (Originally published in 1884 by Forest and Stream.)

Osborn, Minott A. Camp Dudley—the First Fifty Years. Huntington Press, New York, NY. 230 pp. 1934.

Petzoldt, Paul. The Wilderness Handbook. W.W. Norton, New York, NY. 1974.

Roberts, Harry. Movin' Out (Equipment and Techniques for Eastern Hikers.) Stone Wall Press, Lexington, MA. 139 pp. 1975.

Rowsome, Frank Jr. The Bright and Glowing Place. Steven Greene Press, Brattleboro, VT. 212 pp. 1975.

Schmidt, Ernest F. Camping Safety. American Camping Association, Bradford Woods, Martinsville, IN 46151. 43 pp.

Seton, Ernest Thompson. Trail and Camp-Fire Stories. Boy Scouts of America, Supply Division, Melrose Park, IL. 155 pp.

Seton, Ernest Thompson. The Book of Woodcraft and Indian Lore. Doubleday, Garden City, NY. 590 pp. 1925.

Seton, Ernest Thompson. The Birchbark Roll of Woodcraft. A.S. Barnes, Cranbury, NJ. 268 pp. 1931.

Seton, Julia Moss. By a Thousand Fires. Doubleday, Garden City, NY. 271 pp. 1967.

Steffansson, Vilhjalmur. Arctic Manual. (Prepared under the direction of the Chief of the Air Corps.) Macmillan, New York, NY. 556 pp. 1944.

Tacoma Mountain Rescue Unit. Outdoor Living. P.O. Box 696, Tacoma, WA 98401. 56 pp.

U.S. Department of Agriculture. Outdoors USA: The Yearbook of Agriculture. Washington, DC. 408 pp. 1967.

U.S. Department of Agriculture. Backpacking in the National Forest Wilderness. Superintendent of Documents, Washington, DC 20402. 28 pp. 1971.

Van Matre, Steve. Acclimatizing; A Personal and Reflective Approach to a Natural Relationship. American Camping Association, Martinsville, IN 46151. 225 pp. 1974.

Vinal, William "Cap'n Bill" Gould. Nature Recreation. Dover, New York, NY. 310 pp. 1963.

Watts, Alan. Instant Weather Forecasting. Backpacker Books, Main Street, Orwell, VT 05760. 66 pp. 1978.

White, Stewart Edward, The Forest. The Outlook Co. (Out of print). 276 pp. 1903.

Wilkerson, James A. Medicine for Mountaineering. The Mountaineers, 719 Pike Street, Seattle, WA 98101. 368 pp. 1975.

Wood, Robert S. Pleasure Packing. Condor Books, Berkeley, CA. 215 pp. 1972.

INDEX